بسم الله الرحمن الرحيم

Allah intends but to remove all sorts of uncleanness and blemish from you and to purify you with a thorough purification.

Qur'an 33:33

THE JEWELS OF THE AHLUL BAYT

VOLUME II

The Life and Marriage of
FATIMAH AL-ZAHRAH

Luqman al-Andalusi

First published in February 2017 by IHRC Press
Revised Edition, February 2021

Author: Luqman al-Andalusi
General Editor: AH Choudhury
Design & Typeset: Ibrahim Sadikovic

IHRC Press is an imprint of Islamic Human Rights Commission Ltd,
a limited company registered in England and Wales.
Registered office: 202 Preston Road,
Wembley, Middlesex, HA9 8PA, United Kingdom

ISBN 978-1-909853-20-1

Printed by Mega Print, Turkey

Contents

بسم الله الرحمن الرحيم

و صلى الله على سيدنا محمد و آله الطاهرين

The concept of "Holy Family" is prominent in the Qur'an. The Qur'an mentions and highlights many such "Holy Families." In fact, the third Surah of the Qur'an is named after one such family, i.e. Aal-Imran (the Family of Imran). Here Allah ﷻ highlights the virtues of a daughter of two very pious parents. This is Lady Maryam ؑ. Not only is she the daughter of pious parents, but she is also the mother of a pious child, our master Jesus ؑ. In this Surah (and other Surahs), Allah ﷻ details the life of this pious daughter and mother.

Highlighting the status of this and other Holy Families, Allah ﷻ states in Surah Aal-Imran (Ayah 33):

"Indeed, Allah elevated Adam, Noah, and the Family of Abraham and the Family of Imran above the Worlds."

So, it naturally follows that the Family of the Seal of the Prophets, our master Muhammad ﷺ would also fall under that category. Indeed, the Qur'an confirms this by stating (Surah Ahzab, Ayah 33):

"O people of the Prophetic household! Allah intends but to remove all sorts of uncleanness and blemish from you and to purify you with a thorough purification."

And so, in this purified Muhammadan household, we

meet another chaste daughter and mother – Fatimah al-Zahrah – the most beloved *daughter* of Sayyiduna Muhammad ﷺ, and *mother* of the two princes of Paradise, Hasan and Husayn.

If Maryam was raised by parents praised in the Qur'an such as Imran and Hannah, then Fatimah was raised by the one to whom the Qur'an was revealed, and the first believer in it!

If Maryam raised a pious son such as Jesus, who spent his youth calling towards God, then Fatimah raised the two pious sons about whom the Prophet of God ﷺ stated: "Hasan and Husayn are the leaders of the Youth of Paradise"!

Indeed, many Ulama have stated that Sayyidah Fatimah is the greatest woman that ever walked on the face of this Earth, just as her father ﷺ was the greatest man that ever lived.

And this is for good reason. Firstly, due to the clear hadith that states:

"Fatimah is the leader of all the women of Paradise."
(Narrated by Bukhari)

Secondly, due to her connection with the best of Creation ﷺ.

There is a hadith that says:

"Many men achieved perfection but only four women: Asiyah bint Muzahim the wife of Pharoah (adoptive mother of Moses), Maryam bint Imran (mother of Jesus), Khadijah bint Khuwaylid (the wife of Muhammad), and Fatimah the daughter of Muhammad."
(Narrated by Abu-Nu'aym, al-Hakim and Tabarani)

Now, if one compares these four honourable women, then Fatimah certainly surpasses the first two due to her connection with Sayyiduna Muhammad ﷺ, who is without a doubt the superior of our master Jesus عليه السلام and our master Moses عليه السلام.

But what about Khadijah عليها السلام? Is Fatimah the superior of her mother as well?

The scholars answer in the affirmative. This is because while Khadijah عليها السلام was the daughter of polytheist parents, Fatimah عليها السلام was the daughter of Muhammad ﷺ and Khadijah عليها السلام. She was raised up by the best parents that ever lived!

So, can there be a greater woman than Sayyidah Fatimah al-Zahrah al-Batul?

The purest daughter of the best of creation ﷺ!

Our master, the gnostic Sidi Ahmad al-Tijani رضي الله عنه, stated that Fatimah عليها السلام was the first *Qutb* (supreme saint) in this Ummah after the death of the Messenger of Allah ﷺ. And none less than Imam Malik held the position that Sayyidah Fatimah عليها السلام was superior to all the *Sahabah,* due to being the flesh and blood of the Messenger of Allah ﷺ. Even the most senior Sahabah respected her status and rank.

Sayyiduna Abu Bakr رضي الله عنه told her: "Indeed O Fatimah, your pleasure is more dearer to me than the pleasure of my own family members."

Sayyiduna Umar رضي الله عنه told her: "O Fatimah, there was no one we loved more than your Father, and there is no one after him we love more than you."

So! Herewith we present to you a beautiful bouquet of flowers from the Garden of Fatimah عليها السلام, compiled by one of the lovers of the *Ahlul Bayt* عليهم السلام, in an age where loving them is dangerous and ignoring them is in vogue.

But! Who can wipe away the memory of the daughter of Muhammad ﷺ and wife of Ali?

The mother of Hasan, Husayn and Zaynab! She remains the beloved of the Ummah forever!

May the peace and salutations of Allah be upon them all, and may Allah reward the compiler on behalf of them. Ameen.

Shaykh Fakhruddin Owaisi al-Madani
Cape of Good Hope, South Africa

لي خمسة أطفي بها حر الوباء الحاطمة

المصطفى و المرتضى و ابناهما و فاطمة

November 2016 / Safar 1438

Publishers Note

Sayyidah Fatimah holds a unique place in Islam and in the hearts of Muslims. Not only was she the daughter of the best of creation, the wife of the Lion of Allah and the mother of the leaders of the youth of paradise, she is a source of inspiration and guidance for all Muslims.

Sayyidah Fatimah's role encompasses every facet of Islam and she is an example for all men and women. Her devotion to Allah was absolute. Her care for her father was such that he referred to her as her father's mother. She was a pillar of strength for her father and her family in the face of oppression and tribulation. Her strength allowed her to stand up to the tyrants of Quraysh as they tormented her beloved father. Her renunciation of the world is an example for us today. She sacrificed her own worldly comforts to serve the poor and needy. In this regard Allah revealed the following verse about her and those, who like her, sacrifice all for the sake of Allah:

> ***"And feed with food the needy, the orphan and the prisoner, for love of Him."*** (Q.76:8)

These sublime qualities were the result of her upbringing at the hands of Sayyiduna Rasul Allah ﷺ and Sayyidah Khadijah. Her personality was moulded by these two great figures in the early years of Islam. She learnt what it meant to be Muslim by watching the sacrifices made by her family and great figures like Sumayyah, Bilal and Abu Bakr. The result is the figure we know and love, a woman of great integrity, piety and strength.

Sayyidah Fatimah is a beacon, a light guiding us towards the Qur'an and sunnah. In a world of materialism, of celebrity role models and growing secularism, she provides us with an alternative role model. An example steeped in the love of Allah and his Messenger ﷺ. A guide that teaches us to serve others, to sacrifice for Allah, and to devote ourselves to those around us.

Much can be said about Sayyidah Fatimah and her virtues. This work attempts to capture and present some of her virtues. I pray that we all benefit from her example – that her example provides guidance to those of us who are lost, hope for those of us who are broken, and inspiration for the lovers of Allah and His Messenger ﷺ.

> *People! I have left among you that which if you take hold of, you will never go astray: the Book of Allah and my household.* — Sayyiduna Rasul Allah ﷺ

AHC
London, UK
03 Safar 1438 A.H.

Introduction

Assalaamu Alaykum

Do you find yourself unable to find books that are fair and balanced in relation to the beloved family of the Messenger of Allah ﷺ? This is an issue that has been brought to the attention of many students of knowledge and teachers alike. Therefore it was decided that this issue needed to be addressed, as many students and teachers find themselves blindly following the current systems of sectarian hate. Some do not rely upon sound narrations and will relate anything and everything; this allows false stories to be accepted. On the other hand, you will find some who are so strict in sticking to the actual text of books that they may reject sound information relayed through time without the need for books, or they reject some weak narrations that can still be implemented. These are just some of many problems facing our ummah.

For far too long we have fought about the way to implement Islam within our personal and communal lives. We do this based upon the mindset of one doctrine over the other; with adherents on both sides acting outside of the model of Prophetic mercy and forgiveness. Each side sees themselves as the best, the victors and upholders of the sunnah.

This mindset and implementation of Islam has brought about many wars and numerous unnecessary killings. So, why are we doing this to one another? Why have we hurt one another based upon our own narrow belief systems?

This way of being is unfair to everyone, including the Prophet ﷺ and his family; that we have acted in such an inhumane manner is an injustice to all of humanity. We need to bring in love and mercy as our guides in this world and what we do not need, especially in these times, is in-fighting over doctrine.

In an attempt to battle against this narrow mentality on both sides of the fence, The Jewels of the Ahlul Bayt series is a non-sectarian book series that hopes to bring fairness and justice into the equation.

In this book we hope that you will learn how to benefit from the life and example of the daughter of the Prophet Muhammad ﷺ – Fatimah al-Zahrah.

It hopes to shed light on the brighter side of life, highlighting the love among the Prophetic household, the sacrifice they made for humanity, and the good example shown by their actions and words.

So, where can we begin when it comes to the beloved daughter of the Messenger of Allah ﷺ? Among the virtues of our queen and master – Sayyidah Fatimah al-Zahrah – is that she is known as the Qutb among the Aqtaab, the purest of the pure, the most pious among the pious, the leader of the women of Paradise, the wife of our master Mawla Ali, and the mother of the leaders of Paradise – may Allah ﷻ send His Divine Peace upon her. The list could go on and on.

Fatimah al-Zahrah is such a great personality that the scholar of Madinah, Imam Malik ibn Anas named his own daughter Fatimah after her. Many greats would follow in this trend and to this day Fatimah is a name used worldwide. This is an honor from Allah for the most beloved woman of humanity – Sayyidah Fatimah al-Zahrah.

It is as the companion Hudayfah narrated, *"Fatimah is the chief of the women of Paradise, and al-Hasan and al-Husayn are the chiefs of the youths of the people of Paradise."*

The Prophet Muhammad ﷺ saw this glory and high rank within his daughter and could only connect her to one who was like herself, therefore he said, *"There would not be one sufficient for Fatimah if Allah had not created Ali."*

From their beloved union came the two lights, the exemplars of the Prophet's ﷺ mercy and compassion. The Prophet ﷺ himself said, *"For al-Hasan, he is my over-powering personality and leadership and as for al-Husayn, he is my courage and generosity."*

Sayyidah Fatimah al-Zahrah, being such a beautiful example to her children, brought about these good traits within her family, as she is the guide towards beauty and graciousness.

She lived in this beautiful manner throughout her life, helping the Prophet ﷺ throughout his life in even the most trying of times. She is the one he ﷺ shared his inner most secrets with at his time of passing from this world.

She herself, upon the time of her passing, "was washed for burial by her husband Ali ibn Abi Talib, who also prayed over her and buried her by night."

This work has been made possible due to the support from a myriad of beloved teachers and students. I would firstly like to thank my beloved wife, Ustadha Aliyah, for putting up with this student of knowledge as he dove into the deep oceans of knowledge. I would like to thank SKT Welfare, Sacred Knowledge, Madina Institute USA, the Nasirry family, the Darab family, Ruslan Moore, Islamic Human Rights Commission, Madani Book Propagation, Said Bak, and Rasyid Hussein. There are many others, too many to list, but whose help, support and dua's have helped in the fruition of this endevour. May Allah ﷻ bless each of them abundantly.

May Allah ﷻ send peace and divine blessings upon her beloved soul.

All praise is due to Allah ﷻ and with Allah is the success.

Luqman al-Andalusi

Chapter 1:

The Mines of the People of the Cloak (Ahlul-Kisa)

We begin in the name of Allah ﷻ, the Most-Gracious, the Most-Merciful, knowing that all praise is due to Him alone.

May the peace and blessings of Allah ﷻ be upon the Prophet Muhammad ﷺ, his family and companions.

During this journey within the mines of the people of the cloak (*Ahlul-Kisa*), we shall come across many jewels from the Prophet Muhammad ﷺ, Sayyidah Fatimah al-Zahrah, Sayyiduna Ali ibn Abi Talib and Imams al-Hasan and al-Husayn. These blessed individuals are mentioned within the famous hadith of the cloak that will be spoken of in various sections within this book.[1]

For the time being, let us observe the fact that the Qur'an exalts the people of the cloak and the family of the Prophet Muhammad ﷺ in general.

Allah ﷻ revealed the verse of purification (*Ayat al-Tathir*), wherein it reads, ***"O people of the Prophetic household! Allah intends but to remove all sorts of uncleanness and blemish from you and to purify you with a thorough purification."*** (Q.33:33)

Within the sunnah of the Prophet Muhammad ﷺ there is an authentic narration on the authority of Umar, the son of Abu Salamah, who narrated, "This verse [of purification, Q.33:33] was revealed in the house of Umm Salamah and after the revelation of this verse the Messenger of Allah ﷺ called for al-Hasan, al-Husayn and Sayyidah Fatimah and made them sit in front of himself. Then he called for Ali and made him sit behind his back. Then the Messenger of Allah ﷺ covered himself and everyone else up within the cloak and said, *'These are the people of my (inner) house. O Allah! Keep all impurities away from them and purify them with a thorough purification.'* "[2]

In another narration Umm Salamah said, "then I entered my head into the room and asked, 'O Messenger of Allah ﷺ am I also with you?' He replied, *'You are in your place and (do not worry) you are moving toward a good ending.'* "[3]

Aisha al-Siddiqah reported that the Messenger of Allah ﷺ went out one morning wearing a striped cloak of black camel's hair and that there came al-Hasan ibn Ali. He wrapped him under it, then came al-Husayn and he wrapped him under it along with the other one (al-Hasan). Then came Fatimah and he took her under it and then came Ali and he also took him under it and then he recited the verse of purification (Q.33:33).[4]

What has to be understood is that the love for the people of the cloak is not some strange idea at all; it is something that the famous Imams of Islam have always observed.

For example, regarding the people of the cloak, Imam Abu Idris al-Shafi recited one of the most beautiful poems ever written about the prophetic household as follows:

O household of Allah's Messenger!
Love for you is a duty from Allah
In the Qur'an He sent down
[High glory is yours
And he who has no relation with you,
Has no prayer]. [5]

This love is mandatory upon us all. This is proven within the Qur'an, where Allah ﷻ commands the Messenger of Allah ﷺ to say, ***"Tell (them)! I do not ask of you any reward for it, except that you have love for my close family; and whoever earns good, We shall increase that good therein; truly, Allah is Forgiving, the One who Appreciates."*** (Q.42:23)

Jabir ibn Abdullah al-Ansari said, "One day, a nomad came to the Prophet ﷺ and said, 'O Muhammad, offer Islam to me!' The Prophet ﷺ said, *'You should bear witness that there is no god but Allah, Who is One and Only with no partner, and that Muhammad is His slave and messenger.'* The nomad asked, 'Do you ask me for a recompense for it?' The Prophet ﷺ said, *'No, except love to the relatives.'* The nomad asked, 'My relatives or your relatives?' The Prophet ﷺ said, *'My relatives.'* The nomad said to the Prophet ﷺ, 'Give me your hand to pay homage to you. On whoever does not love you and does not love your relatives the curse of Allah be!' The Prophet ﷺ replied, *'Ameen!'* "[6]

The Messenger of Allah ﷺ also said, *"Love Allah for what He nourishes you with of His blessings, and love me due to [this] love of Allah, and love my Ahlul Bayt due to [your having] love of me."*[7]

Imam Zayn al-Abidin (Ali ibn al-Husayn) narrates that the Messenger of Allah ﷺ said, *"Make the love of our family obligatory, for whoever meets Allah ﷻ having love for us shall enter paradise with our intercession; and by He in whose Hand is my life, no deed will benefit a servant except by recognizing our rights."*[8]

The family of the Prophet ﷺ in general are the elite of humanity and this is proven by the fact that the Messenger of Allah ﷺ said, *"Indeed my elite, those whom I lean towards, are the people of my inner house and my close ones are the helpers of Madinah [Ansar], so forgive those who do wrong from them and accept from those who do good from them."*[9]

Sayyiduna Ali ibn Abi Talib narrates that the Messenger of Allah ﷺ said, *"I will recompense on the Day of Judgement the one who fulfills the rights of even one of my family members,"*[10] and, *"Whoever lends a hand to the people of my family has a reward on the Day of Judgement."*[11]

To reiterate, the Messenger of Allah ﷺ tells us to love Allah ﷻ because of what He provides for us from among His blessings, to love the Messenger of Allah ﷺ due to this love of Allah ﷻ, and have love for the people of his house (*Ahlul Bayt*) due to this love for the Messenger of Allah ﷺ.

The reward for this is great, for the Messenger of Allah ﷺ said, *"Whoever loves me will be with me in the Garden."*[12]

The Messenger of Allah ﷺ also said, *"My Prophetic household and I are a tree in paradise whose branches came to this world to benefit it. Thus whoso will, may choose a path unto his Lord."*[13]

O Allah ﷻ allow us to be firmly rooted within this tree and allow us to benefit from the fruits of its harvests. Ameen!

"Don't you see how Allah makes a simile in the form of a beneficial word, like a good tree with stable roots and its crown in the sky: it produces its fruits at all times, by permission of its Lord." (Q.14:24-25)

So with this intention we ask Allah ﷻ to accept our love of the Prophetic household (*Ahlul Bayt*) by means of the blessings, mercy and light of the Prophet Muhammad ﷺ, his family and companions.

It is important indeed to renew this intention at all times, in order to allow our actions to be within the scope of the Qur'an and sunnah. The love for Allah ﷻ and His Messenger ﷺ must be a top priority in one's life.

A proof of this can be seen in the saying of the Messenger of Allah ﷺ, *"A servant will not be a believer unless he loves me more than his own soul, and loves my family [Ahlul Bayt] more than his own soul, even to the point that this love exceeds that (love) given towards his own family."*[14]

Much more can be said, yet brevity is sunnah and with Allah ﷻ is the success.

Chapter 2:

The Mine of the Ark (Safinah)

In this section we have come upon a waterway within the mine of the *Ahlul-Kisa*, thus we must board the ark / *Safinah* of salvation in order to arrive safely at our final destination. Many gems and jewels are waiting to be discovered during this part of our exploration.

Allah ﷻ says, ***"And indeed We have honored the Children of Adam, and We have carried them on land and sea, and have provided them with the lawful good things, and have preferred them above many of those whom We have created with a marked preferment."*** (Q.17:70)

We now board the ship of the *Ahlul Bayt* and ***"Surely, this is a reminder; so whoever wills, let him take a way to his Lord"***. (Q.76:29)

Sayyiduna Ali ibn Abi Talib said, "By Allah, we are for this community [*ummah*] what the Ark [*safinah*] of the Prophet Nuh was to his people, and we the family of the Messenger of Allah ﷺ are for this community what the Gate of Repentance [*Hitta*] was for the Children of Israel."[15] [16]

This hadith of Sayyiduna Ali is very important. To become more familiar with the gate of *Hitta*, Allah ﷻ speaks about it in the Qur'an. He says, ***"And when We said: Enter this city; then eat from it a plentiful food wherever you wish, and enter the gate making obeisance, and ask for forgiveness [Hitta]. We will forgive you of your wrongs and give more to those who do good (to others)."*** (Q.2:58)

In another narration, Anas ibn Malik related the Prophet ﷺ as saying, *"Surely the likeness of my family is similar to (the Prophet) Nuh's ark, whoever boards it will attain salvation and whoever remains behind is drowned."*[17]

The Prophet Muhammad ﷺ himself said, *"We serve as the ark of salvation. Whoever holds fast to this ark will reach salvation and whoever deviates from it will be cast into perdition. Whoever wants Allah to grant him something should resort to the Ahlul Bayt."*[18][19]

Imam al-Shafi recited a beautiful poem wherein he said, "I boarded the ark of salvation in the name of Allah." This ark is truly crystallized within the family of the Prophet Muhammad ﷺ – the seal of the prophets.

Much more can be said, yet brevity is sunnah and with Allah ﷻ is the success.

Chapter 3:

Mine of Light –
The Light of the Prophet's ﷺ Eye

We now enter into the third mine within the mines of the people of the cloak. All praise be to Allah ﷻ, if we look at the prophetic hadiths we will see that the light of the Prophet's ﷺ eye is his beloved daughter Fatimah al-Zahrah[20]. The Prophet ﷺ himself said, *"The most beloved of my family to me is Fatimah."*[21]

Sayyidah Fatimah al-Zahrah is such a great figure within Islam that the Messenger of Allah ﷺ informed her, *"Fatimah, you will be the first amongst my family to enter Paradise after me."*[22]

This news came directly from Allah ﷻ and His angels as is related by the Messenger of Allah ﷺ. He says, *"An Angel in the heavens who had never seen me before requested permission from Allah to see me and Allah granted him permission. He told me the good news that Fatimah is the leader of all women in my nation."*[23]

To be more specific, there is a hadith on the authority of Hudayfah who narrates that the Messenger of Allah ﷺ said, *"There is an angel who before tonight has never come down to earth, he asked permission from his Lord to offer greetings of peace to me and to deliver the good news to me that Fatimah is the leader of all women of Paradise and al-Hasan and al-Husayn are the leaders of the youth of Paradise."*[24]

There is also another jewel related on the authority of Zayd ibn Ali, who relates on the authority of his forefathers and they, on the authority of Sayyiduna Ali ibn Abi Talib, who narrates that the Messenger of Allah ﷺ informed Sayyidah Fatimah, *"Allah, after viewing all the humans on earth selected your father (al-Mustafa) and made him a prophet (and messenger). Again Allah viewed the world and selected your husband as my brother and spiritual inheritor. Then after viewing the universe for the third time, He selected you and your mother and appointed both of you as leaders of all womenfolk. Allah glanced at the universe a fourth time and selected both your sons and conferred on them the honour of being the leaders of all youths of Paradise."*[25]

We now turn our attention to the Mine of Light. In numerous verses of the Qur'an, Allah speaks of the Messenger of Allah ﷺ being a light.

In one such verse, Allah ﷻ says, ***"O Prophet! We have sent you as a witness, a giver of glad tidings and a warner, one who calls to Allah by His permission and a lamp spreading light."*** (Q.33:45-46)

The companion Ka'b ibn Zuhayr composed the following poetry in praise of the Prophet ﷺ:

The Messenger is surely a sword
from whose flash light is sought,
One of the swords of God,
an Indian[26] blade unsheathed...,[27]

Upon hearing this poem, the Prophet ﷺ took his mantle (Burda) off his shoulders and put it on Ka'b's, signaling his approval of the poem.

Shaykh Abd al-Ghani al-Nablusi explained this reality when he said, "The Prophet ﷺ is the universal leader of all, and how could he not be when all things were created out of his light as has been stated in the sound hadith."[28]

Allah ﷻ also says, ***"There has come to you a light from Allah and a clear Book."*** (Q.5:1)[29]

Abu Hurayrah narrates, "I have not seen anyone more beautiful than the Messenger of Allah ﷺ, it was as if the sun is shining upon his face. I have not seen anyone quicker in his walking than the Messenger of Allah ﷺ, it was as if the earth was made easy for him (to tread). We would tire ourselves out (following him) while he would not struggle."[30]

This light from Allah ﷻ being spoken of in the above verses is indeed the Messenger of Allah ﷺ; and Sayyidah Fatimah in her manners and persona is a manifestation of this light of prophecy, as she emulates her father in every matter.

In another verse Allah says, ***"Allah is the light of the heavens and the earth; a likeness of His light is as a niche in which is a lamp, the lamp is in a glass,"*** (Q.25:35) and we ***"Give the kinsman his due".*** (Q.17:26)

Therefore, O Fatimah! By the light of Allah ﷻ and His Messenger ﷺ, your mother Khadijah, Maryam bint Imran and Asiyah, we take you as a means of approach to our Lord and in doing so, we intend to follow the light of the straight path – for the straight path is illuminated by your beloved father and is the one who makes everything within the heavens and the earth luminous.

As we travel a little deeper within these mines, please take notice of the fact that Sayyidah Fatimah al-Zahrah literally comes from the light of the Prophet Muhammad ﷺ.

Sayyiduna Ali ibn Abi Talib said, "Allah was and there was nothing with Him, and the first thing which He created was the light of His Beloved, before He created water, or the Throne, or the Footstool, or the Tablet, or the Pen, or Paradise, or the Fire, or the Veils and the Clouds, or Adam and Eve, by four thousand years."[31]

Imam Zayn al-Abidin relates from his father al-Husayn who narrates from his father Ali ibn Abi Talib that the Messenger of Allah ﷺ said, *"I was a light in the presence of Allah, the Exalted and Majestic, fourteen thousand years before the creation of Adam. When Allah created Adam, He placed that light in his loins, and I was continually transmitted from loin to loin until I settled in the loins of Abd al-Mutallib."*[32]

Shaykh Abd al-Qadir al-Jilani explains the above when he says:

> The Muhammadan soul [*al-Ruh al-Muhammadiyyah*] is therefore the quintessence of all created things and the first of them and their origin, as the Prophet ﷺ said: "I am from Allah and the believers are from me, and Allah created all souls from me in the spiritual world and He did so in the best form." It is the name of the totality of mankind in that primordial world, and after its creation by four thousand years, Allah created the Throne from the light of Muhammad ﷺ himself and from it the rest of creation.[33]

Allah ﷻ says, ***"When your Lord drew forth from the children of Adam [from their loins] their descendants, and made them testify concerning themselves (saying), 'Am I not your Lord?' They said, 'Yes, indeed!'"*** (Q.7:172)[34]

This natural disposition is discussed by Imam al-Tabari in his explanation of the verse ***"I [shaytan] will order them to change the nature created by Allah"*** (Q.4:119), where he explained, "The natural disposition [*fitrah*] is what is spoken of here and it is the Islamic way of life given by Allah."

This is also the sacred connection between the prophets and the Messenger of Allah ﷺ.

Sayyiduna Ali ibn Abi Talib said, "Allah never sent a prophet but after taking his pledge that if Muhammad ﷺ were sent in his lifetime, he would believe in and support him." [35]

Sa'id ibn al-Jubayr said, "The children of Adam differed over who was the dearest of creatures to Allah; some of them saying the greatest is Adam because Allah created him with His own Hands and commanded His angels to prostrate to him (Adam). Other scholars have said: No, the angels are the ones who do not disobey Allah [nor are they able, thus they are better within this stance]. They went to Adam (to enquire about this) and Adam replied: 'Truly, I am the dearest of all creatures except that when the spirit was breathed into me, it had hardly reached my feet before I sat up fully and the Throne glimmered before me and I gazed at it; lo and behold! There was written upon it, Muhammad is the Messenger of Allah ﷺ. For, in all reality, he is the dearest of all creatures to Allah Almighty!' "[36]

Imam Hasan al-Basri said, "Allah took the pledge from the prophets that they would believe in each other," and this statement does not contradict what Ali stated.[37]

Therefore, we say that the Prophet Muhammad ﷺ is the final prophet, he is the greatest imam, who if he existed in any time period, is deserving of being obeyed, over and above any other prophet.

The main proof for this is that the Prophet Muhammad ﷺ led all the other prophets in prayer during the night of *Isra'* when they gathered in *Bayt al-Maqdis* (Jerusalem). He is also the intercessor on the Day of Gathering, when the Lord comes to judge between His servants.

This is the very famous station of *al-Maqam al-Mahmud* referred to in the Qur'an (Q.17:79). This station, in fact, is what the beloved Prophet Muhammad ﷺ deserves; it is a responsibility which the prophets and messengers will decline to assume. However, the beloved Prophet Muhammad ﷺ will carry the task of intercession, may the peace and blessings of Allah ﷻ be upon him, his family and companions.[38]

As can be seen, the greatness of the Messenger of Allah ﷺ is apparent for the world to see. We must extract these jewels and show them to humanity in order to benefit each of our communities. Keeping them safe upon the ark is a great task indeed. May Allah give us all success.

Another jewel we can extract from this mine is the reality of the Prophet Muhammad ﷺ being the result of an accepted supplication of his forefather Ibrahim.

The Messenger of Allah ﷺ himself said, "I am the invocation of my father, Ibrahim, and the glad tidings of my brother, Isa. My mother had a vision that a light emanated from her and lit up the palaces of Syria."[39] [40]

The invocation being spoken of is the invocation (*dua*) of the prophet Ibrahim, ***"Our Lord, and send among them a messenger from themselves who will recite to them Your verses and teach them the***

Book and wisdom and purify them. Indeed, You are the Exalted in Might, the Wise." (Q.2:129)

The proof of the Prophet Muhammad ﷺ being the glad tidings of Isa is stated within the Qur'an as well, wherein Allah ﷻ says, ***"And [mention] when Isa, the son of Maryam, said, 'O children of Israel, indeed I am the messenger of Allah to you confirming what came before me of the Torah and bringing good tidings of a messenger to come after me, whose name is Ahmad.' "*** (Q.61:6)

In the Book of Deuteronomy it reads, "I will raise up for them a prophet from among their brethren like you, and will put My words in his mouth [the Qur'an]; and he shall speak to them all that I command him."[41]

This explanation is consistent with what Allah ﷻ says in the Qur'an, ***"Nor does he (Muhammad) speak of his own desire. It is but an Inspiration that is inspired [unto him]."*** (Q.53:3-4)

Elsewhere within the Bible it reads, "And the book is delivered to him that is not learned, saying, 'Read this, I pray thee': and he saith, 'I am not learned.' "[42]

This of course can be related back to the first verse of the Qur'an to be revealed, ***"Iqra!"*** (Q.96:1)

The Messenger of Allah ﷺ also said, *"My similitude in comparison with the other prophets before me is that of a man who has built a house nicely and beautifully, except for a place of one brick in a corner. The people go about it and wonder at its beauty, but say, 'Would that this brick be put in its place!' So I am that brick, and I am the Seal of the Prophets."*[43]

"And We did certainly give Moses the Torah and followed up after him with messengers. And We gave Isa, the son of Maryam, clear proofs and supported him with the holy spirit. But is it [not] that every time a messenger came to you, [O Children of Israel], with what your souls did not desire, you were arrogant? And a party you denied and another party you killed." (Q.2:87)

Much more can be said, yet brevity is sunnah and with Allah ﷻ is the success.

Chapter 4:

The Mine of Sayyidah Maryam

We now arrive at the Mine of Mayram bint Imran, the mother of the Prophet Isa. This Prophetic light we are seeing around us is most definitely reflected within the life of Sayyidah Fatimah, the greatest mother, queen, and saint of all time. Maryam and Fatimah are mirrors of one another. In this chapter we will see the similarities between Sayyidah Fatimah and Sayyidah Maryam.

With that noted, we bear witness to needing the spiritual lights of Sayyidah Maryam, Khadijah, Asiyah, and Fatimah in our lives, as their blessed examples and character are perfect models of success to emulate.

The spiritual chivalry of Sayyidah Fatimah, Khadijah and Maryam is similar to when Imam al-Sulami says in his *Kitab al-Futuwwa*:

> Jesus the son of Mary shone with the purest of light of spiritual chivalry [*Futuwwa*] and he became known as the spirit [*Ruh*] and the Messiah through it. Entire victory was given to the Prophet Muhammad ﷺ and

> his two companions Abu Bakr and Umar, along with Ali ibn Abi Talib who became the guardians of it (spiritual chivalry).[44]

Sayyiduna Ali ibn Abi Talib narrates, "I heard the Prophet ﷺ saying, *'Maryam, the daughter of Imran, was the best among the women (of the world of her time) and Khadijah is the best amongst the women.'*"[45]

We also bear witness that Sayyidah Fatimah al-Zahrah is the greatest woman of this life and the next. O Fatimah! You are the fruition of your mother Sayyidah Khadijah, the close friend of Sayyidah Fidda and a light of our mother Sayyidah Maryam. You, O Fatimah! You are the perfected light of womanhood!

Sayyidah Fatimah's connection to Sayyidah Maryam is deep indeed. Allah ﷻ says, ***"Maryam, Allah has chosen you and purified you. He has chosen you over all other women."*** (Q.3:42)

The explanation of the verse ***"Maryam, Allah has chosen you and purified you..."*** is beautifully given by Hafidh ibn Kathir who explains, "What is meant by this, is that she (Maryam) was specifically chosen to be the greatest among the women of her own lifetime. It does not mean that she outranks all women. The meaning of it is similar to when Allah says, ***'Musa: I have chosen you above all of mankind.'*** (Q.7:144) This does not mean that Musa outranks the Messenger of Allah (al-Mustafa) ﷺ."[46]

Many verses and prophetic sayings such as these confuse some people who claim that all of the prophets and messengers are equal in rank. Yet, after careful analysis, the people of remembrance say that according to the sound text, the proofs point to the fact that the best of creation is al-Mustafa ﷺ and this is according to the consensus [*ijma*] of the Muslim community.

One may ask, so how would we reconcile the above with the statement of Allah, ***"We make no distinction between the Messengers"*** (Q.2:285)?

To answer this, it should be known that this non-distinction is only in regard to the message of Islam itself that each prophet or messenger delivered, and has nothing to do with the rank of the Prophet ﷺ.

For example, Allah ﷻ says, *"**We did not send any messenger before you except with the inspiration that there is no god except Me; (and that) you shall worship Me alone.**"* (Q.16:36) This shows the equality and uniformity in the message that the prophets and messengers were delivering.

The following verse shows that indeed some have a higher standing than others throughout all of creation, ***"We have made some messengers to excel over others; to some of them Allah spoke [directly]; others He raised to degrees (of honour); and to Isa, the son of Maryam, We gave clear proofs and evidences, and supported him with Ruh-ul Qudus [Jibreel / Gabriel]."*** (Q.2:253)

Therefore, with the above knowledge, we now know that the Prophet Ibrahim, Musa, Ayyub, or any other prophet is not of a higher rank or degree than the seal of the prophets, meaning the Prophet Muhammad – al-Mustafa ﷺ.

The sayings praising them are well known and are called the Hadith of Honor. Many of the companions of the Prophet Muhammad ﷺ and his family have similar sayings mentioning them being the leaders of paradise, the first to enter paradise, etc., but this does not mean that they outrank the Prophet Muhammad ﷺ.

To stay on course, another important verse of the Qur'an showing the great status of Sayyidah Maryam is, ***"Every time he entered her private room [al-Mihrab] (to visit) her [Maryam], he found her supplied with sustenance. He said, 'O Maryam! From where have you got this?' She said, 'From Allah.' Truly, Allah provides sustenance to whom he wills, without limit."*** (Q.3:37)

The significance of all of this is that the traits described about Sayyidah Maryam also apply to Fatimah al-Zahrah. If you look at both of their lives in detail you will see that Sayyidah Fatimah al-Zahrah is similar to Sayyidah Maryam, the mother of Isa/Jesus, in both her character and charitable ways.

On one occasion the Messenger of Allah ﷺ drew four lines on the ground, then he said, *"Do you know what this is?"* We the companions said, "Allah and His messenger know best." The Messenger of Allah ﷺ said, *"The best of the women of paradise are Khadijah bint Khuwaylid, Fatimah bint Muhammad, Asiyah bint Mazahim, and Maryam bint Imran."*[47]

Is not Fatimah al-Zahrah purified just like Sayyidah Maryam? Allah ﷻ says, ***"O people of the Prophetic household! Allah intends but to remove all sorts of uncleanness and blemish from you and to purify you with a thorough purification."*** (Q.33:33)[48]

Allamah Iqbal mentions that while Sayyidah Maryam is distinguished for having given birth to Sayyiduna Isa, Sayyidah Fatimah al-Zahrah is distinguished with the following three honours (crowns of excellence):

Firstly, she is the 'sweet delight of him who came a mercy to all living things' and this is significant for us because he is the leader of the prophets and the whole universe.

Secondly, she is the wife of the Lion of Allah, he being the one who is the master of all the believers.

Thirdly, she is the mother of Imam al-Hasan who is the leader of the caravan of love and Imam al-Husayn the lord of all of earth's saints.[49]

Much more can be said, yet brevity is sunnah and with Allah ﷻ is the success.

Chapter 5:

The Birth of Sayyidah Fatimah al-Zahrah and Sayyiduna Ali

Now let's journey into the deep Mine of the life of Sayyidah Fatimah al-Zahrah. The first jewel we see is a verse of the Qur'an wherein Allah ﷻ says, ***"The grace of Allah and His blessings be upon you, O You people of the house!"*** (Q.11:73) and another is, ***"(As for) Those who say, Our Lord is Allah, then continue in the right way, the angels descend upon them, saying: Fear not, nor be grieved."*** (Q.41:30)

It is related that the Prophet ﷺ said, *"Truly, Allah has protected my daughter Fatimah and her children and those who love them from the Hellfire, and that is why she is named Fatimah."*[50]

A virtue of both Sayyiduna Ali ibn Abi Talib[51] and Sayyidah Fatimah, the daughter of the Messenger of Allah ﷺ, is that they were born in the city of Makkah. Fatimah was born to the greatest of creation, the Prophet Muhammad ﷺ, and Khadijah[52]; while Ali was born to the famous Fatimah bint Asad and Abu Talib, the leader of the Banu Hashim.

Sayyidah Fatimah bint Asad said, "When Ali was born, the Messenger of Allah ﷺ gave him this name and made him suck his tongue. He dropped his saliva in the mouth of the baby and put his tongue in his mouth. Sucking the tongue, the baby slept. On the second day we searched for a foster mother, but Ali took away his mouth from the bosom of the women. We thought of Muhammad ﷺ. He put his tongue in the mouth of the baby who then slept soundly. This went on till Allah desired it to be so."[53]

Sayyidah Fatimah al-Zahrah is said to have been born in the year 605 CE. Whilst there is some dispute as to the exact date, the majority say that she was born during the same year as the re-building of the Ka'bah in Makkah after a flood, and Allah ﷻ always knows best.[54]

This honor of being born in Makkah was also given to Sayyiduna Ali; his connection to the city and to the Ka'bah is great indeed.

In regard to the many virtues of the Ka'bah itself, Allah ﷻ says, ***"Most certainly, the first House of worship appointed for mankind was that at Bakkah (Makkah), full of blessing, and a guidance for all of creation."*** (Q.3:96)

The significance of being born in Makkah is that Allah ﷻ, His angels, prophets, messengers and saints bless the city at all times. So much so, that Allah swears by the city of Makkah in the Qur'an. He says, ***"I swear by this city, Makkah – And you, [O Muhammad ﷺ], are free of restriction in this city."*** (Q.90:1-2)

This is an oath of Allah ﷻ that He makes by the sanctity of Makkah, due to the fact that living in it puts one into a state of ihram, itself a form of sanctity. Allah also says, ***"And by this city of security (Makkah)."*** (Q.95:3)

We should pray and wish to live within this sanctuary and to pass away in a blessed land (Madinah, Makkah and al-Quds being the best). Imam al-Nawawi commented on this by saying, "It is recommended [*mustahabb*] to seek to die in a virtuous land."[55]

Much more can be said, yet brevity is sunnah and with Allah ﷻ is the success.

Chapter 6:

The Mine of Prophetic Beauty

We now enter the mine of Prophetic Beauty, and within this mine we shall explore the features of the Prophet Muhammad ﷺ, Sayyidah Fatimah al-Zahrah and her husband Ali ibn Abi Talib.

In relation to the Prophet Muhammad's ﷺ features it is narrated, "The Messenger of Allah (al-Mustafa) ﷺ, was the most handsome of all people, and had the best appearance."[56]

Once a man asked, "Was the face of the Prophet ﷺ as long as a sword?" He was told, "No, but it was as wide as the sun and the moon."[57] In another narration it reads, "The Messenger of Allah ﷺ was neither completely white, nor was he extremely dark and he had a touch of rose upon him."[58]

Sayyiduna Ali ibn Abi Talib described the Prophet ﷺ for us when he said, "The Prophet ﷺ was not extremely tall nor short. His palms and feet were fully fleshed, his head was large and his joints were large. A thin line of hair ran from his chest to his navel. When he would walk, he would lean forward slightly; such that it would appear that he was descending from an elevated plain. I did not see his like, neither before him or after him."[59]

These features are within Sayyidah Fatimah al-Zahrah herself, "Nobody showed more resemblance to the Prophet ﷺ than al-Hasan (ibn Ali ibn Abi Talib) and Fatimah (bint Muhammad)."[60]

It is related, "Fatimah was like a moon on its full night, or the sun covered by no clouds. She was fair skinned [wheatish complexion], with a touch of rose color on her face, her hair was black and she had the beautiful features of the Messenger of Allah ﷺ."[61]

Umm al-Mu'minin[62], Aisha al-Siddiqah, narrated, "I never saw anyone who resembled the Prophet ﷺ in his physical appearance, his gestures and mannerisms more than his daughter Fatimah, even in how she stood and sat. When she would come to visit him, he would sit her down in his place."[63]

Much more can be said, yet brevity is sunnah and with Allah ﷻ is the success.

Chapter 7:

The Mine of Innocence

We now enter the Mine of Innocence and within this mine we shall explore the excellent values with which Sayyidah Fatimah al-Zahrah was raised, and we do this with the intention of pleasing Allah ﷻ and his Messenger ﷺ and all that they love. May Allah ﷻ make us all among the lovers. Ameen.

Sayyiduna Ali ibn Abi Talib narrated that the Prophet ﷺ loved Fatimah with all of his heart and soul and said, *"Fatimah is a part of me. Therefore, whoever angers her has angered me."*[64]

We see that indeed the Prophet's ﷺ love is intense, and can be seen in his statement, *"Indeed, Fatimah is my fruitful branch; whatever makes her happy also makes me happy and whatever hurts her, hurts me."*[65]

It is also related that whenever Sayyidah Fatimah was hurting, the Messenger of Allah ﷺ would come to her aid and would say out of love for his daughter, *"Oh Fatimah! May my mother and father be sacrificed for you."*[66]

The Prophet ﷺ, being the best of creation, was also the best parent. During his lifetime, whenever Sayyidah Fatimah would visit the Prophet ﷺ, "he would welcome her and then he would stand up for her, kiss her, take her hand and bring her forward until he made her sit in his place."[67]

Aisha al-Siddiqah narrates that when Sayyidah Fatimah used to visit the Prophet ﷺ, he used to stand up to welcome her, kiss her and by holding her hand used to seat her where he was sitting. When the Prophet ﷺ visited Fatimah's house, she welcomed him by standing up and kissing the blessed hand of the Prophet ﷺ.[68]

The actions and good nature of Sayyidah Fatimah al-Zahrah – as taught to her by her beloved mother and father – made her the manifestation of the verses of the Qur'an, ***"Be good and dutiful to your parents,"*** (Q.6:151) and, ***"Say not to them a word of disrespect, nor shout at them but address them in terms of honor."*** (Q.17:23)

Sayyidah Fatimah treated her parents with utmost respect at all times and in every place; indeed she was the epitome of the Prophetic sunnah itself.

Her emulation of the Prophet Muhammad's ﷺ good treatment of her mother Khadijah is what influenced the good behaviour of the young Fatimah from a young age. These good manners and actions of the Messenger of Allah ﷺ towards his family were a way for him to teach his daughter the reality of the following sayings:

"The most complete of the believers in faith are those with the best character, and the best of you are the best in behavior to their women."[69]

"The best of you is he who is the best to his family, and I am the best to my family."[70]

Allah ﷻ says, ***"And lower unto them the wing of submission and humility through mercy, and say: 'My Lord! Bestow on them [my parents] Your Mercy as they did care for me when I was small.' Your Lord knows best what is in your inner-selves. If you are righteous, truly, He is Ever Most Forgiving to those who turn unto Him in obedience, and in repentance."*** (Q.17:23-25)

As if he is the interpretation of the verse himself, Sayyiduna Ali ibn Abi Talib also served and protected the Prophet Muhammad ﷺ at all times.

He speaks of the care the Prophet ﷺ gave him when he said, "I was still a young child when the Prophet ﷺ took me into his custody. I would stick by him at all times and he used to feed me, and because of this companionship, when I grew a little older, he saw that I never told a lie, nor have I ever tried to deceive people. In regard to me, the Prophet ﷺ was like a guiding star and I used to follow his actions and deeds very carefully. I was attached to him like a newborn camel attached to its mother. He always taught me about and emphasized the importance of high moral values, and he advised me to make sure that I follow them [these moral values]. There was a time every year, that he would spend a few days at the grotto of mount Hira and I used to go with him. I was his only companion then and none else could meet him at Hira. It was there that I used to see the light of revelation, and used to smell the fragrance of prophethood. Once the Prophet ﷺ told me, *'Ali! You have attained a very eminent place. This is because you see what I see and you hear what I hear.'*"[71]

It is also worth mentioning that within pre-Islamic Arabian culture most people were burying their newborn daughters alive and would treat their wives as slaves, cattle and personal property.

With the help of Allah ﷻ, the Prophet ﷺ and his wife Khadijah helped to put a stop to this cruel treatment of women; in fact, it is due to their hnourable actions that many women have rights today that may have othwerwise been usurped. Khadijah herself had to undergo ill treatment from the women of the Quraysh when she married the Prophet Muhammad ﷺ. Khadijah, being a lady of great wealth, was now looked down upon for not marrying into royalty or money. She was effectively cast out, and her comfort was Allah ﷻ, His Messenger ﷺ, and her family.

The Purity of Sayyidah Fatimah

The innocence of Sayyidah Fatimah was such that the Prophet ﷺ declared, *"Fatimah has protected her chastity and purity in such a way that Allah has forbidden the fire for her and her family."*[72]

Her modesty and purity can be seen in her response to the Messenger of Allah ﷺ when he once asked her, *"Which are the best women?"* She replied, "those whom men do not see and those who do not see men." The Messenger of Allah ﷺ was delighted and embraced her saying, ***"offspring, one of the other."*** (Q.3:34)[73]

And this purity and chastity will continue in the hereafter as Allah's Messenger ﷺ has stated, *"On the Day of Resurrection a herald will announce from behind a veil: 'Oh People of the Great Assembly! Lower your gazes until Fatimah, the daughter of Muhammad, passes.' "*[74]

Much more can be said, yet brevity is sunnah and with Allah ﷻ is the success.

Chapter 8:

The Mine of the Year of Revelation (610 CE)

We now enter into the Mine of Revelation and the year is 610 CE. As we enter this mine, let's take note of the fact that even before revelation, and despite her young age (some reports saying as young as five), Sayyidah Fatimah would accompany her blessed mother to the cave of Hira on the spiritual and physical journey of bringing food and comfort to her father. Her blessed mother was in fact, through these treks, teaching Sayyidah Fatimah how to develop strength and endurance. Fatimah was witnessing firsthand the lengths a good wife will go to for a good husband. The physical exertions that both Sayyidah Khadijah and the young Fatimah had to go through just to give the Messenger of Allah ﷺ food and water is a sign of great love itself.

Sayyiduna Ali ibn Abi Talib is known to have accompanied the Prophet ﷺ to the cave of Hira. As mentioned earlier, Sayyiduna Ali ibn Abi Talib himself said, "It was there that I used to see the light of revelation, and used to smell the fragrance of prophethood. Once the Prophet ﷺ told me, *'Ali! You have attained a very eminent place. This is because you see what I see and you hear what I hear.'* "[75]

The year 610 CE is an important year for many reasons; one is that in this year, during the month of Ramadan, the angel Jibreel came to Prophet Muhammad ﷺ with the revelation of the Qur'an.

While the Prophet ﷺ was in retreat within the cave of Hira, Jibreel grabbed him firmly and said, "Read!" The Prophet ﷺ surprised by this, responded *"But, I cannot read"*. This happened numerous times and then Jibreel said, ***"Read! In the Name of your Lord Who has created (all that exists). He has created man from a clot. Read! And your Lord is the Most Generous. Who has taught (the writing) by the pen. He has taught man that which he knew not."*** (Q.96:1-5)[76]

After this first great event of revelation, the Prophet ﷺ rushed back home to Sayyidah Khadijah[77 78] and told her what had happened. After listening to her beloved husband, Sayyidah Khadijah – herself having already learnt about religion, the earlier prophets and the angel Jibreel – at once supported the Prophet Muhammad ﷺ and accepted Islam.[79]

The most significant thing about the Prophet Muhammad ﷺ and Sayyidah Khadijah's marriage was that she became the first person to accept Islam. She, without hesitation, submitted herself to the will of Allah ﷻ and his Messenger ﷺ with complete faith.

She reminded him who he was and encouraged and comforted him, telling the Messenger of Allah ﷺ, "I swear by God He would never abuse you. You maintain family ties, you are hospitable to guests, you support the weak, provide for the poor and help out when tragedy strikes."[80]

Sayyidah Khadijah truly is among the greatest women in the history of the world and a beautiful example for both her daughter and women in general.

The Prophet ﷺ attests to this fact when he says concerning his beloved wife Khadijah, *"She believed in me while the people disbelieved in me and she trusted in me while the people were lying about me and she helped and comforted me in person and in wealth when the people would not. Allah Provided me with children by her, and He did not do so with others."*[81 82]

Sayyidah Khadijah was a source of great strength for the Prophet ﷺ:

> Khadijah was Mohammed's first convert. From the moment of his first call, until her death nine years later, she never faltered. Whenever he encountered mockery or contradiction, he was sure, when he returned home in the evening, to find a cheerful and loving comforter. She was always ready by her confident equanimity to restore his courage and to lighten the burden of his fears.[83]

The love story between the Prophet ﷺ and Sayyidah Khadijah is so inspiring, and although Sayyidah Fatimah al-Zahrah was still young, she was not blind to how impressive her mother and father's relationship was.

The amount of love the Prophet ﷺ had for his wife Sayyidah Khadijah is a testament to the ethics and morals of Islam itself. It is this love story that shapes the love story of Ali and Fatimah.

Aisha al-Siddiqah said, "One day, the Messenger of Allah ﷺ mentioned Khadijah affectionately, so I was carried away by jealousy and said about her what I should not have said. It was then that his face changed colour in a way I never saw it change except when he was receiving revelation, so I realized what I had done and felt overwhelmed by regret to the extent that I could not help uttering these words, 'O Lord! If You remove the anger of Your messenger right now, I pledge not to ever speak ill of her again in my life.' Having seen that he forgave me and then related some of her virtues to me."[84]

May the elevated status of Sayyidah Khadijah be echoed throughout the mines of righteousness. Ameen.

Much more can be said, yet brevity is sunnah and with Allah ﷻ is the success.

Chapter 9:

The Mine of Struggle

We now enter the Mine of Struggle. Within this mine we shall look at the struggles of the Prophetic household, including Sayyidah Fatimah and Sayyiduna Ali, and how it shaped their lives. Sayyidah Fatimah witnessed all of the early Qurayshi oppression towards her family and the believers in general.

During the first year of revelation in 610 CE, after hearing about the Prophet Muhammad ﷺ receiving revelation, many prominent members of Makkan society became Muslim and submitted themselves to the religion of Islam.

Irritated by this, one day, Abu Jahl was sitting with the leaders of the Quraysh in front of the Ka'bah, and Sayyidah Fatimah al-Zahrah overheard them saying, "We will kill Muhammad for rejecting our idols and bringing this new religion, we just have to figure out a way to do it." Sayyidah Fatimah, shaken by this, immediately rushed back to tell her father what she had heard and he told her not to worry and to *"have faith in Allah, for He is my Protector"*.

Another of the oppressors who frustrated the Messenger of Allah ﷺ, Abu Talib and Sayyidah Fatimah was Walid ibn al-Mughirah.

Allah ﷻ mentions this Qurayshi leader negatively within several verses of the Qur'an. Walid was the one who recommended that the Quraysh call our beloved Prophet ﷺ a sorcerer; someone who had brought a message by which he separated a man from his father, brother, wife or family. The Quraysh went to such extremes that they appointed certain members of the tribe to lie in wait for pilgrims coming into Makkah in order to warn them about the dangers of the message brought by our beloved Prophet Muhammad ﷺ. Walid himself knew the truth of Islam and yet he did not accept it for personal and selfish reasons. There was a time when the Qur'an even touched the heart of Walid, yet Allah ﷻ guides whom He wills at the times He wills and with Allah ﷻ is the success.

For these disgraceful actions carried out by Walid against the Messenger of Allah ﷺ and his beloved family, Allah ﷻ revealed many verses about him. Allah ﷻ says:

> ***Let Me deal with one I created as an individual.***
> ***I provided him with an abundance of wealth.***
> ***And children to behold.***
> ***I made everything easy for him.***
> ***Yet, he is greedy for more.***
> ***He stubbornly refused to accept Our verses.***
> ***I will increasingly punish him.***
> ***For he reflected, then decided.***
> ***Miserable is what he decided.***
> ***Miserable indeed is what he decided.***
> ***He looked.***
> ***He frowned and scowled.***
> ***Then he turned away arrogantly.***
> ***He said, "This is but clever magic of old!***
> ***This is man-made speech."*** (Q.74:11-25)

On another occasion the Prophet Muhammad ﷺ was sitting with Walid ibn al-Mughirah by the Ka'bah when al-Nadir ibn al-Harith came and sat with them among the assembly of the Quraysh. When the beloved Prophet Muhammad ﷺ spoke, al-Nadir would always interrupt him. On this specific occasion, the Prophet ﷺ responded until he silenced him again. Then the Prophet ﷺ read to them all:

> ***You and what you worship besides Allah are fuel for Hell. You will go down into it.***
> ***If those had really been gods, they would not have gone down into it. Each will be in it timelessly, for ever.***
> ***There will be sighing for them in it and they will not be able to hear.*** (Q.21:98-100)

After the Prophet ﷺ had left, Abdullah ibn al-Zibara al-Sahmi arrived. Walid said to him, "By Allah, al-Nadir could not stand up to Muhammad just now, and he alleged that we and our gods are fuel for Hell." Abdullah replied, "If I had found him, I would have refuted him. Ask Muhammad, 'Is everything that is worshipped besides Allah in hell with those who worship it?' We worship the angels; the Jews worship Uzair; and the Christians worship Jesus the son of Mary." Walid and those with him in the assembly marveled at Abdullah's words and thought that he had argued convincingly. When the Messenger of Allah ﷺ was told of this he replied, *"Everyone who wishes to be worshipped to the exclusion of Allah will be with those who worship him. They worship only shayateen and those they have been ordered to be worshipped."*[85] Ibn al-Zibara said, "You have been dumbfounded by the Lord of this building [meaning the Ka'bah]. Do you not claim that the angels are righteous servants and that Jesus is a righteous servant and that Uzair is a righteous servant? Well, the Banu Mulayh worship the angels, the Christians worship Jesus and the Jews worship Uzair." Upon hearing this, the people of Makkah cried out [of jubilation] believing the Prophet ﷺ was defeated, and so Allah ﷻ revealed, ***"Those who have received kindness from us in the past [Jesus, Uzair etc] will be removed far from it [hell], and will not hear its sound and they will abide eternally in their heart's desire [in Paradise]."*** (Q.21:101-102)

On another occasion Walid said, "Does God send down revelations to Muhammad and ignore me, the greatest chief of Quraysh, to say nothing of Abu Masud Amr ibn Umayr al-Thaqafi, the chief of Thaqif, we being the great ones of Taif and Makkah?"[86] Allah ﷻ immediately responded to this by saying:

> ***And they say: 'Why is not this Qur'an sent down to some great man of the two towns (Makkah and Ta'if)?'***
> ***Is it they who would portion out the Mercy of your***

Lord? It is We Who portion out between them their livelihood in this world, and We raised some of them above others in ranks, so that some may employ others in their work. But the Mercy (Paradise) of your Lord (O Muhammad!) is better than the (wealth of this world) which they amass. (Q.43:31-32)

On another occasion, while the Prophet ﷺ was circumambulating the Ka'bah, Walid approached him along with al-Aswad ibn al-Muttalib ibn Asad ibn Abd al-Uzza, Umayyah ibn Khalaf and al-Aas ibn Wa'il to offer him a proposition. They said, "O Muhammad, come on! We'll worship what you do if you'll worship what we do. Let's just co-operate, you and us, in the whole thing!"[87]

The response to this proposition was given by Allah ﷻ in Surah al-Kafirun:

Say, O disbelievers!
I do not worship what you worship,
and you do not worship what I worship,
and I do not worship what you worship,
and you do not worship what I worship;
You have your way of life (Deen) and I have mine.
(Q.109:1-6)[88]

On another occasion, the Prophet Muhammad ﷺ passed by Walid, Umayyah ibn Khalaf and Abu Jahl. They reviled and mocked him, and you could see that it was affecting him in his person, so Allah ﷻ revealed, *"(Do not worry) Messengers have been mocked before you, but that which they mocked at (always) hemmed them in."* (Q.6:10)[89]

Sayyidah Fatimah grew up witnessing all of these events and remained steadfast in the face of this oppression, and her resolve to follow Islam never faltered.

Much more can be said, yet brevity is sunnah and with Allah ﷻ is the success.

Chapter 10:

The Mine of Admonition

We now enter into the Mine of Admonition. It is the year 613 CE and Sayyidah Fatimah is eight years old.

Allah ﷻ says, ***"Proclaim what you have been ordered and turn away from the polytheists. We will surely protect you against the mockers, who set up another god alongside Allah. In the end they will know."*** (Q.15:94-96)

To give some context to the times we are in: there had been a break in revelation for a time, and during these times the Muslims would go to the mountains and hills of Safa to pray in secret. The house of al-Arqam was then established for the purpose of worship, reflection and meditation.

Jabir ibn Abdullah al-Ansari narrates, while talking about the period of pause in revelation, that the Prophet ﷺ said, *"While I was walking, all of a sudden I heard a voice from heaven. I looked up and saw the same angel who had visited me at the cave of Hira sitting on a chair between the sky and the earth. I got afraid of him and came back home and said 'Wrap me (in blankets)' and then Allah revealed,* ***'O you covered in your cloak, arise and warn.'*** *After this revelation came strongly and regularly."*[90]

Allah ﷻ decreed the year 613 CE to be the year that He commanded the Prophet Muhammad ﷺ to invite others to Islam publicly. This command is very clear and it was this verse, ***"O you covered in your cloak, arise and warn"*** (Q.74:1-2) that instructed the Prophet ﷺ to approach everyone, even the powerful tribes of Quraysh, with the message of Islam.

On one occasion, the Prophet ﷺ gathered all of the tribes of Quraysh at the top of the mountain and shouted, *"O my people! Woe to you from an evil that is coming in the morning."* He called on each of the tribes by their name and then asked them, *"If I told you all that the enemy was going to attack you in the morning, or in the evening, would you all believe me?"* and they said, "We have never experienced a lie from you." So he said, *"Indeed, I am a warner (sent) to you all (warning you) before the coming of a severe torment."*

Abu Lahab, the uncle of the Prophet ﷺ replied to this declaration by saying, "Have you gathered us for this? Tabba Laka (may you perish)." In response to this disgraceful comment, Allah ﷻ revealed Surah al-Masad against Abu Lahab and his wife, Umm Jamil, because of their harsh treatment of the Prophet ﷺ. Abu Lahab was furious about the news of this revelation and made it his mission to destroy the entire family of the Prophet Muhammad ﷺ.[91]

As was noted, Sayyidah Fatimah al-Zahrah, although still young, saw the persecution of her father and the believers. She witnessed Abu Lahab and the Quraysh abusing and mocking her father. She saw her own sisters mistreated, and their marriages broken apart because of the hurtful and disgraceful actions of Umm Jamil, Abu Lahab and his sons, which is discussed further in the next section.

Much more can be said, yet brevity is sunnah and with Allah ﷻ is the success.

Chapter 11:

The Mine of Freedom

As we enter the Mine of Freedom, we are still in the year 613 CE. This is the year that Abu Lahab forced his sons Utbah and Utaybah to divorce their wives. This move was meant to disgrace the family of the Prophet Muhammad ﷺ, however it did not work.

Abu Lahab caused the divorces of Sayydah Fatimah's sisters – Sayyidah Ruqayyah and Sayyidah Umm Kulthum – by tempting his sons with the most beautiful women of the Quraysh. Utbah divorced Ruqayyah right away, and Utaybah also had his marriage contract voided with Umm Kulthum.

Imam al-Tabari said, "Umm Kulthum was also married to Abu Lahab's son Utaybah, but they never consummated the marriage," and Allah ﷻ knows best.[92]

Imam ibn Sa'd also relates this story in his *Tabaqat,* saying that Abu Lahab threatened to not speak to Utaybah unless he divorced Umm Kulthum. Imam ibn Sa'd states, "When the Messenger of Allah ﷺ was sent and Allah ﷻ sent down, ***'Perish the hands of Abu Lahab,'*** (Q.111:1) his father, Abu Lahab, said to him, 'My head is unlawful to your head if you do not divorce his daughter.' So he parted from her without having consummated the marriage."[93]

Her maternal brother, Hind ibn Abi Hala,[94] once asked the Messenger of Allah ﷺ, "Why did you separate Umm Kulthum from Utaybah?" The Messenger of Allah ﷺ replied, *"Allah did not allow me to marry her to a person who is not going to paradise."*[95]

Both Sayyidah Ruqayyah and Umm Kulthum were divorced from their husbands due to Abu Lahab's animosity towards the Prophet ﷺ and Islam. However, they went on to happily marry again. In fact, they both married Uthman ibn Affan[96] with Ruqayyah marrying him first in 615 CE and after her passing, Umm Kulthum happily married him in 624 CE.

The elder sister of Sayyidah Fatimah – Sayyidah Zaynab – was also going through her own tribulations. Indeed, her story could be a book in and of itself, as she was deeply in love with her husband Abu al-Aas ibn al-Rabi.

Sayyidah Zaynab became a Muslim as soon as her father declared himself as the Messenger of Allah ﷺ. The family wanted her husband to also become Muslim, however he refused to do so at the time.

The Quraysh – having already succeeded in causing the divorces of Sayyidah Umm Kulthum and Sayyidah Ruqayyah – were now set on pressuring Abu al-Aas to divorce Sayyidah Zaynab, saying the same as they had before, "Leave your wife and we will marry you to any Quraysh woman you desire."[97] This was to no avail because he loved his wife, just as she loved him and they did not want anyone other than each other. He replied to Quraysh, "No, by God! I will not leave her, and I do not want any other woman from Quraysh for my wife." The Prophet Muhammad ﷺ was impressed by Abu al-Aas' love for his daughter and because he had no jurisdiction over Makkah at the time, he let the matter be and allowed the marriage to continue. Sayyidah Zaynab even stayed in Makkah to be with her husband when the Muslims migrated to Madinah.

At the Battle of Badr, Abu al-Aas was captured along with other Makkans who were fighting against the Muslims. Many of the Makkans were sending gold to ransom their loved ones held by

Muslims. Sayyidah Zaynab sent a necklace of hers (which Sayyidah Khadijah had owned and given to her when she married Abu al-Aas). When the Messenger of Allah ﷺ saw it, he was moved by this and asked his companions, "If you consider that you should free her prisoner for her and return to her what belongs to her, (it will be well)." They agreed and the Messenger of Allah ﷺ made an agreement with Abu al-Aas that on his return to Makkah he should let Sayyidah Zaynab come to Madinah.

Abu al-Aas kept his promise, and on his return he sent Sayyidah Zaynab to Madinah with his brother, Kinana. On their way to Madinah they were stopped by some of the men of Quraysh, who were infuriated that she was being sent to her father so soon after the defeat at Badr – they felt this was further humiliation being heaped on them. They brandished their swords against Sayyidah Zaynab, their aggression and hostility was so fierce that Sayyidah Zaynab, being pregnant at the time, miscarried her child. It was agreed by the men who stopped her that she would go back to Makkah, and when things had quietened down she could return to her father. Some time later, Sayyidah Zaynab was allowed to quietly leave Makkah and join her father in Madinah.[98]

Much more can be said, yet brevity is sunnah and with Allah ﷻ is the success.

Chapter 12:

The Mine of Patience Among Persecution

The year is still 613 CE and the Quraysh are increasing their persecution of the believers. Abu Lahab, Abu Jahl and Abu Sufyan were masterminding numerous attempts on the Prophet's ﷺ life and were also trying to extinguish any semblance of Islam within Makkah, in order to protect their power-structure and the economic perks of worshipping idols. Before Islam, the Ka'bah was used to house the idols of the Quraysh. However, as Allah ﷻ says, ***"They want to extinguish Allah's Light with their mouths, but Allah will not allow except that His Light should be perfected even though the disbelievers hate (it)."*** (Q.9:32)

Abu Jahl and the Quraysh made a pact with one another to not allow any Muslim to pray near the Ka'bah, and there are many instances of them trying to enforce this rule. For example, after warning the Muslims not to pray near the Ka'bah, Abu Jahl stoned the Prophet ﷺ in the marketplace and whenever he ﷺ went outside. In fact, Sayyiduna Ali would have to stand guard, to ward off the stones being thrown by various members of the Quraysh.

Sayyidah Fatimah, Sayyiduna Ali, and the Messenger of Allah ﷺ would frequently be in each others' presence; worshiping, studying and learning together.

Sayyidah Fatimah and Sayyiduna Ali grew up together and went through what is known as *suhbah* (spiritual training and companionship) with the Prophet ﷺ and would go to the different caves and mountains of al-Safa and the surrounding area.

They both acted as guardians of the Prophet ﷺ, with Sayyiduna Ali, being so close to his beloved, that everyone around Ali looked at him as a bodyguard of the Messenger of Allah ﷺ. Sayyiduna Ali, Sayyidah Fatimah and the Prophet ﷺ were attacked on numerous occasions, and each time they successfully saw off their attackers.

Around the year 614-615 CE, the Muslims started the migration to al-Habasha (Abyssinia in Africa). This was also around the time when the three deputations of the Quraysh were sent to Abu Talib in Makkah.

Muhammad ibn Ishaq relates:

> When the apostle saw the affliction of his companions … he said to them: *"If you were to go to Abyssinia (it would be better for you), for the king will not tolerate injustice and it is a friendly country, until such time as Allah shall relieve you from your distress."*[99]

Many companions took the advice of the Messenger of Allah ﷺ and made the migration to Africa. Prominent members of the companions such as Jafar ibn Abi Talib, Ruqayyah (the sister of Sayyidah Fatimah) and Uthman ibn Affan are among those who made the first migration.

Even after the migration, the Quraysh tried to force the return of the believers to Makkah in order to punish them for leaving their religion and ridiculing the Qurayshi gods. They sent ambassadors to the Negus, who tried to shower gifts upon the Negus and then brought their case against the Muslims to him.

However, Jafar ibn Abi Talib won over the heart of the Negus after reciting Surah Maryam to him. Indeed, so impressed was the Negus with Jafar's speech that he refused to return the Muslims to be harmed by ones who did not believe in Allah ﷻ. He subsequently returned all of the gifts back to the Quraysh and told them to leave his land.[100]

Now, after this humiliating return to Makkah, the Quraysh vowed more than ever to end Islam and uproot it from Makkah forever.

They started usurping the properties of the Muslims and removing them from their homes. Some remained steadfast in the face of this adversity, while others kept their faith secret for fear of death.

In spite of this persecution, Bilal ibn Rabah, a slave at the time, was public with his Islam and is amongst those who stood firm and chose to repeat '*ahad*' (the One God) instead of being humiliated by his torturer into calling upon other gods besides Allah ﷻ.[101] This proved to be the best move he could ever have made, for he was freed by Sayyiduna Abu Bakr al-Siddique, became the beloved of the Messenger of Allah ﷺ and the first caller of the *adhan*. His strength in the face of such overwhelming adversity is what has made him a major inspiration to the ummah; someone who reminds us to hold on to our faith no matter what we are faced with.

Even as the Muslims were freeing slaves, the Quraysh attacked the weak followers of the Prophet ﷺ in the most brutal manner and even attacked the inner household of the Prophet ﷺ.

But, after the humiliation the Quraysh felt in Abyssinia and with the slave rebellion reaching new heights in Makkah, the Quraysh felt they now had no other choice but to come to the bargaining table. For example, Sayyiduna Bilal made a huge scene when he would not submit to Ummayah's attempt to make him reject Allah ﷻ, and instead kept repeating, "Ahad, Ahad." Sayyiduna Abu Bakr al-Siddique ended up freeing Bilal and other Muslims as well, may Allah ﷻ reward him with paradise for his service to Islam. Umar ibn al-Khattab would later say concerning Abu Bakr and Bilal, "My master who freed my master."

It was in this highly charged atmosphere that Sayyidah Fatimah grew up. She learnt to be resilient in the face of persecution and hardship.

Much more can be said, yet brevity is sunnah and with Allah ﷻ is the success.

Chapter 13:

The Mine of the Three Deputations

We now enter the Mine of the Three Deputations and we are in the years 614-615 CE.

The Quraysh sent three deputations to the Messenger of Allah ﷺ and Abu Talib to try and convince the Muslims to return to the religion of their forefathers, and for Abu Talib to stop protecting the Prophet Muhammad ﷺ.

The Quraysh had been complaining about the religion of Islam for many years now. In a final attempt to convince Abu Talib of their point of view, the Quraysh brought Ammarah ibn Walid ibn al-Mughirah, and said as quoted by Imam ibn Hisham, "The Quraysh said, 'Your nephew has insulted our gods, called our great men insane and reckoned our fathers to be deviated ones. Therefore, you surrender him to us or else, there shall occur a war between us.' "

Abu Talib replied, "May your mouths be shut forever. I swear by Allah that I shall never surrender him to you."

They also said, "Ammarah ibn Walid ibn al-Mughirah is the most handsome and noble young man among the Quraysh. You may keep him as your son instead of Muhammad and surrender Muhammad to us so that we can kill him. Let us exchange our man with your man."[102]

Abu Talib replied, "Woe be upon you people. May Allah turn your face dark and gloomy. I swear by Allah that you have indeed spoken evil. Do you mean that I should hand over my son to you so that you can kill him and will give me your son in exchange so that I take care of him! I swear by Allah that if I do so, I would be but an evil man."[103]

Thereafter he said, "I would like you to separate the baby-camels from their mother. If the mother camel gets attracted towards the other baby-camels and not her own ones, then, I shall hand over Muhammad to you."[104]

Events such as these made the Quraysh – especially Abu Lahab, Abu Jahl and Abu Sufyan – even more outraged at the Muslims and the new belief system in general, and thus they went to the other leaders of Makkah to convince them that it was now time to threaten Abu Talib as well.

At first, Abu Talib pleaded with his nephew to come to some terms with the Qurayshi leaders. During one instance, Abu Talib said, "Please spare me and yourself, and do not put a greater burden on me than I can bear." The Prophet ﷺ responded to his uncle by saying, *"Oh uncle! By Allah Almighty I swear, even if they should put the sun in my right hand and the moon in my left that I abjure this cause, I shall not do so until Allah has vindicated it or caused me to perish in the process."*[105]

On another occasion, Abu Talib set up a meeting with the tribe of Quraysh and the Prophet ﷺ called them to Islam; this made them even angrier.

This of course, was until Allah ﷻ commanded the Messenger of Allah ﷺ, saying to him, ***"And warn your family members."*** (Q.26:214)

Imam ibn Ishaq explains in his *Seerah Nabawiyyah,* that the Messenger of Allah ﷺ – obeying the command of Allah ﷻ – then asked Ali ibn Abi Talib to gather all of the members of the tribes in the home of his uncle Abu Talib for dinner. Upon this occasion the

Messenger of Allah ﷺ took the opportunity to speak to the other members of his tribe, including the Banu Hashim.

The Messenger of Allah ﷺ said, *"O sons of Abd al-Muttalib, I swear that I do not know of anyone from among the Arabs who has brought anything better than what I have brought. I have brought the goodness of this world and the next and Allah has ordered me to invite you to these precepts and I will befriend one of you to be my brother and my successor."* After this was said, everyone looked around as if they did not care and they really paid no attention to it, other than Sayyiduna Ali ibn Abi Talib, who was the youngest among them. He stood up and said, "O Messenger of Allah ﷺ, I am your helper upon this way."[106]

The Messenger of Allah ﷺ then put his arm around Ali's shoulder and said, *"This brother is my [spiritual] inheritor and my successor among you. Listen to his words and obey his orders."*

This is the event where, "the leaders of the Quraysh laughed and said to Abu Talib that Muhammad has ordered you to obey your son."[107]

The Qurayshi leaders now looked at the whole family as a threat.

As was noted in the above, the Quraysh continued this rhetoric of hatred against the Messenger of Allah ﷺ and anyone who loved and supported him.

Abu Lahab, Abu Jahl and others would tell the people of Makkah, "You see Muhammad is a fraud, nothing comes to him except magic."

Allah ﷻ confirms this when He says, ***"(The Quraysh say) Why has the Qur'an not been vouchsafed to him (Muhammad) in one single whole?"*** (Q.25:32) Allah ﷻ answers the false accusations of the Quraysh, directly in another verse, ***"If We had sent unto you (O Muhammad) a written (message) on parchment, so that they could touch it with their hands, the unbelievers would have been sure to say, 'This is nothing but obvious magic.' "*** (Q.6:7) In another verse it reads, ***"A Qur'an which We have divided (into parts from time to time), in order that you might recite it to people at intervals: We have revealed it by stages (in 23 years)."*** (Q.17:106)

615 CE is the year of heavy persecution from the Qurayshi leaders; it is now five years into the revelation of the Qur'an and the Quraysh were as angry as can be. To release some of this anger, they publicly tortured, humiliated and killed many Muslims, as was the case for Bilal ibn Rabah, Ammar ibn Yasir, Summayah and her husband Yasir. The Prophet ﷺ himself witnessed the family of Yasir being subjected to torture and is known to have said, *"Patience, O family of Yasir! Your meeting-place will be Paradise."* They indeed had patience and their mother Summayah was honored to become the first martyr of Islam.[108]

In this same year, 615 CE, the Prophet ﷺ stood in the place known as al-Hijr, preparing to pray. Alongside him was Sayyidah Fatimah.

Abu Jahl then came up right in front of him and screamed out, "Which of you can bring the entrails of a slaughtered animal and throw it on top of Muhammad?"

A criminal by the name of Uqbah ibn Abi Muayt responded to the call and threw the entrails of an animal upon the shoulders of the Prophet ﷺ while he was still in *sujud* (prostration).

Other leaders of Makkah such as Umayyah ibn Khalaf, Shaybah, and Utbah, were also present and were laughing hysterically at what had just happened.

Sayyidah Fatimah, seeing her father in this condition, removed the entrails from him and then admonished Abu Jahl, asking him how he could do such a thing to his own nephew. He did not respond to this and the Prophet ﷺ then went on to complete his salat while Sayyidah Fatimah stood by him. According to other narrations, they were also being pelted with stones.[109]

In the *Sahihayn*, on the authority of Abdullah ibn Masud, it is narrated that the Prophet ﷺ was praying at the Ka'bah, and Abu Jahl and his companions were sitting there. They said to one another, "Who will bring the intestines of the camel of so and so and put it on Muhammad's back when he prostrates?" So the most wretched of people went and brought it out and waited until the Prophet ﷺ prostrated, then he put it on his back, between his shoulders. I was watching but I could not help him because I did not have any power. They started laughing and leaning against one another (because of their laughter), and the Messenger of Allah ﷺ was prostrating and did not raise his head until Fatimah came and removed it from his back. Then the Messenger of Allah ﷺ raised his head, and said, *'O Allah, deal with the Quraysh,'* three times. They became worried when he prayed against them, because they used to believe that the supplication made in that land would be answered."[110]

Sayyidah Fatimah was furious at the above action and it caused her father discomfort. Sayyiduna Ali ibn Abi Talib narrates that the Prophet ﷺ said to Fatimah, *"Indeed, Allah becomes angry when you are angry and He is pleased when you are pleased."*[111]

The actions the Quraysh were taking were always refuted and rebuked in the Qur'an. The anger of Allah ﷻ in this case was truly upon them.

Much more can be said, yet brevity is sunnah and with Allah ﷻ is the success.

Chapter 14:

The Mine of Those Preventing Others from the Prayer

There were so many incidents where the Quraysh prevented the believers from praying near the Ka'bah. The treatment meted out to the Prophet Muhammad ﷺ and Sayyidah Fatimah, even within the *Haram Sharif*, was disgraceful indeed.

Allah ﷻ revealed the following verse in relation to one of these incidents, ***"Have you seen him (Abu Jahl) who prevents a servant when he prays."*** (Q.96:9)

In the *seerah* and books of *tafsir*, the explanation of the verse is that "Abu Jahl said, 'If I see Muhammad praying at the Ka'bah, I will stomp on his neck.' So this reached the Prophet ﷺ who said, *'If he does so, he will be seized immediately by the angels.'* "

"The Messenger of Allah ﷺ was praying at the Maqam of Ibrahim, when Abu Jahl and Hisham passed by him and said, 'O Muhammad! Haven't I prevented you from this.' He threatened the Prophet ﷺ and thus, the Messenger of Allah ﷺ became angry with him and reprimanded him. Then Abu Jahl said, 'O Muhammad! What can you threaten me with, by Allah, I have the most kinsmen in this valley with me in the largest numbers.' "[112]

Then Allah ﷻ revealed, ***"Let him call upon his council. We call out the guards of Hell!"*** (Q.96:17-18)

Abdullah ibn Abbas said, "If Abu Jahl had called his people, the angels of torment would have seized him at that very instant."[113]

On another occasion, the Quraysh sent Uqbah to attack the Prophet ﷺ and he got close to him and started to strangle the Prophet ﷺ with his own clothes, right in front Sayyidah Fatimah. When she saw this happening, she screamed at the top of her lungs for help and Sayyiduna Abu Bakr al-Siddique was the first to rush to the scene and he managed to free the Prophet ﷺ.

While he was doing so, he asked them, "Why would you kill a man who says, 'My Lord is Allah?' "

When Sayyiduna Abu Bakr said this, they once again fell into a rage and beat him in front of everyone for supporting Islam. He accepted this willingly and said that the Prophet ﷺ was his beloved friend and brother – his only concern was that the Messenger of Allah ﷺ was safe.

According to Imam ibn Hisham, "On another occasion, Uqbah spat in the face of the Messenger of Allah ﷺ at the behest and incitement of his friend Ubayy ibn Khalaf, and (because of this disrespect) Allah ﷻ revealed at that moment, ***'Certainly he led me astray from the Reminder after it had come to me, and Satan is a deserter of man,'*** (Q.25:29) regarding both Ubay and Uqbah."[114]

According to Muhammad ibn Ishaq, "Ubayy used to have serious influence over Uqbah and when he heard that Uqbah had listened to the Qur'an from the Messenger of Allah ﷺ, he swore that he would never speak to him if he ever did it again. He also pressured him into spitting in the face of the Messenger of Allah ﷺ. Uqbah indeed carried this out and this is why Allah ﷻ revealed these verses against them."[115]

Once again, these events were witnessed by Sayyidah Fatimah and had an impact on her. She would have felt as everyone else did at being persecuted by the Quraysh. It is worth noting that the Prophet ﷺ said, *"Fatimah is part of my body, whoever hurts her, hurts me,"*[116] and *"Fatimah is a part of me, whoever hurts her, hurts me and whoever puts her in difficulty, puts me in difficulty."*[117]

Much more can be said, yet brevity is sunnah and with Allah ﷻ is the success.

Chapter 15:

The Mine of Perseverance

As we enter the Mine of Perseverance, it is now the year 616 CE, and this is the year of the beginning of the boycott of the Banu Hashim and Muttalib.

During these hard times, Sayyidah Fatimah's service to Allah ﷻ and his Messenger ﷺ speaks volumes.

The backdrop to this was that Sayyiduna Hamzah and Sayyiduna Umar ibn al-Khattab had accepted Islam. Both were strong, brave and powerful men. This scared the common people among the pagans of Makkah and they called upon the leaders of the Quraysh to take military action against the Muslims.

The leadership of Quraysh decided not to take military action, but instead decided to boycott the community, both socially and economically. Even the most basic necessities such as food and water were withheld from the believers, and if food and drink were found, the prices were excessively inflated.

Imam ibn Hisham speaks of the sanctions being carefully planned and put into writing. A parchment was put up and sealed with three stamps, and then when "they all swore by it, the record was hung up in the Ka'bah". [118]

The boycott enforced by the Quraysh lasted three years in the Valley of Abu Talib (*Shi'b Abi Talib*) and, "The boycott was so rigorously enforced at times, that in the first few months the Muslims had to eat the leaves of acacia trees and the cries of the children could be heard throughout the valley."[119]

Sayyidah Fatimah was approximately eleven years of age when the boycott began. Sayyiduna Ali himself was young and had the duty of going out near the city, at the risk of death, to get water, food and other essential goods needed for his family and supporters. Sayyidah Khadijah would also give him gold to buy whatever was needed for the community. She spent her money until her last *dinar* ran out. Truly, she was the best wife or mother that the Messenger of Allah ﷺ or Sayyidah Fatimah could ever ask for.

Allah ﷻ always provides for the believers and this is shown by the fact that the Banu Hashim still had some good hearted people in Makkah trying to help them.

One of the friends of Abu Talib was Hisham ibn Amr al-Aamiri, who was also related to Banu Hashim via his mother. He was highly esteemed by his people. He risked his life and limbs to bring food and water for the Banu Hashim as often as he could. This is described by ibn Ishaq:

> ... when these two clans were in their quarter, he used to bring a camel laden with food by night and then, when he had got it to the mouth of the alley, he took off its halter, gave it a whack on the side, and sent it running into the alley to them. He would do the same thing another time, bringing clothes for them.[120]

There were others also supporting Banu Hashim, like Abul Bukhtari and Hakim ibn Hizam, who was the nephew of Sayyidah Khadijah.

They helped bring in the necessary water and goods needed for both adults and children until Abu Jahl figured out what they were doing. Abu Jahl threatened them and said he would confiscate their camel and goods if they continued supporting those in the valley.

Abul Bukhtari, although not Muslim himself, tried to force his way past Abu Jahl on the basis that it was inhumane to stand by and watch the oppression against Banu Hashim continue in front of their own eyes. He feared this may lead to other tribes being treated in a similar manner as Banu Hashim. Abul Bukhtari and Abu Jahl went on to have an intense argument, followed by a full-blown fist fight.[121]

Hisham ibn Amr al-Aamiri, Abul Bukhtari and Hakim ibn Hizam not only fought and argued with Abu Jahl and Quraysh, they also supported Banu Hashim with their wealth, risking their own lives in the process.

As this was going on, the family of the Messenger of Allah ﷺ steadfastly remained by his side and Fatimah showed her dedication to Islam by serving everyone around her. The boycott and lack of food did of course affect her physical health.

The boycott became so bad that providing food and clothing was not enough; the boycott just needed to be ended altogether. Hisham ibn Amr took it upon himself to find a way to challenge the boycott.

The story is discussed by ibn Ishaq:

> He (Hisham ibn Amr) went to Zuhayr ibn Abu Umayyah ibn al-Mughirah, whose mother was Atika daughter of Abd al-Muttalib, and said: 'Are you content to eat food and wear clothes while you know of the condition of your maternal uncles? They cannot buy or sell or inter-marry. By God, if they were the uncles of Abul Hakam ibn Hisham (Abu Jahl), and you asked him to do what he has asked you to do, he would never agree to it.' He (Zuhayr) said, 'Confound you, Hisham, what can I do? I am only one man. By Allah, if I had another man to back me, I would soon annul it.' He said, 'I have found a man – myself.' 'Find another,' said he. So Hisham went to al-Mutim ibn Adiy and said, 'Are you content that two clans of Banu Abd Manaf should perish while you look on consenting to follow Quraysh? You will find that they

> will soon do the same with you.' He (Mutim) made the same reply as Zuhayr and demanded a fourth man. So Hisham went to Abul Bukhtari ibn Hisham who asked for a fifth man, and then to Zama'a ibn al-Aswad ibn al-Muttalib.[122]

Alhamdulillah, they managed to challenge and successfully overturn the boycott. One of the miracles witnessed during the ending of the boycott was that when they went inside the Ka'bah to rip up the boycott document, the only bit of the parchment that remained were the words: *"In your Name, O Allah!"* Everything else had been eaten by termites.

After the destruction of the document that nullified the boycott, Mutim ibn Adi entered the valley with his tribe fully armed, and escorted the Messenger of Allah ﷺ and his family back to Makkah.

The ending of the boycott only brought a short respite, as more tests were to follow,

> "Soon after the siege of Shi'b Bani Hashim was lifted, the Prophet and Fatimah and her sisters went through the trauma of losing their beloved Khadijah. She had fallen ill during the siege. Ten years had passed since Muhammad declared himself to be the Messenger of Allah. It was about the same time that the Prophet lost his greatest supporter and defender, his uncle Abi Talib. The disbelievers became bolder as they thought he was 'helpless.' Fatimah, from a tender age, was facing all these troubles and experiencing them first hand side by side with her father. It was also at this time that the Prophet went to Ta'if with the Message of Islam. The people there were like the Makkans; they welcomed him with stones and he left Ta'if injured and bleeding. But he did not curse these inhospitable and cruel people; on the other hand he prayed to Allah to guide them to the right path. Umm Kulthoom and Fatimah were very upset and started weeping when they saw his condition. He affectionately wiped away their tears and consoled them. He said it was inevitable that Allah would help to spread His religion and make it triumph against all odds. Easier times were bound to follow the hard and difficult days."[123]

The boycott was one of the toughest hardships the Muslims had to endure and it was indeed a time of extreme hardship for the Messenger of Allah ﷺ. However, as Allah ﷻ says, ***"Verily with every hardship comes ease, most definitely with every hardship comes ease."*** (Q.94:5-6)[124]

Muhammad Haykal talks about the hardships faced by the Prophet ﷺ and his family:

> It is nearly impossible for us to imagine the intensity and extent of the efforts which Quraysh spent in its struggle against Muhammad, or its perseverance during many long years in that struggle. The Quraysh threatened Muhammad and his relatives, especially his uncles. It ridiculed him and his message, and it insulted him as well as his followers. It commissioned its poets to revile him with their sharpest wits and to direct their most caustic sting against his preaching. It inflicted injury and harm on his person and on the persons of his followers. It offered him bribes of money, of royalty and power, of all that which satisfies the most fastidious among men. It not only banished and dispersed his followers from their own country but injured them in their trade and commerce while impoverishing them. It warned him and his followers that war with all its tragedies would befall them. As a last resort, it began a boycott of them designed to starve them.[125]

The beautiful example of Sayyidah Fatimah's life within this particular struggle is that she, along with Sayyiduna Ali, were the ones who would attend to the sick and help seek out food for everyone. Sayyiduna Ali himself would meet up with those in Makkah brave enough to deliver food and goods to them in the valley.

Sayyidah Khadijah, as has been noted, played an integral part in the survival of the Muslims, for she was the one who funded the community until her very last *dinar* was spent. Prices were so inflated that everyone had no choice but to buy overpriced food and water. Thus, by means of the virtuous actions of the Prophet ﷺ, Khadijah, Fatimah and Ali, the difficult times within the Valley of Abu Talib were a whole lot easier.

Imam al-Tabari (ibn Jarir), related from Abdullah ibn Abbas:

> When Abu Talib, the uncle of the Messenger of Allah ﷺ fell sick, the elders of Quraysh, including Abu Jahl, visited him and said, "Your nephew insults our gods. Do justice to us and stop him from insulting them. If he does so then we will leave him and his God alone in return." The Messenger of Allah ﷺ kept saying, "Just say 'La Ilaha Illa Allah." The Quraysh elders were disgusted when they heard this, and when Abu Talib would not reprimand him, they turned their backs dusting their garments, as is the practice of the Arabs when rejecting something. They then said, "Does he want that we give up all our gods and only worship his One God? This is really an amazing thing!"

The rejection of their offer by the Messenger of Allah ﷺ was to tell them (Quraysh), as commanded by Allah ﷻ, ***"Say, 'Indeed, my prayer, my rites of sacrifice, my living and my dying are for Allah, Lord of the worlds. No partner has He. And this I have been commanded, and I am the first [among you] of the Muslims.' "*** (Q.6:162-163)

Much more can be said, yet brevity is sunnah and with Allah ﷻ is the success.

Chapter 16:

The Mine of Umm Abiha (The Mother of her Father)

As we enter the mine of *Umm Abiha,* it should be noted that she was described as such, for she was truly a trustworthy guardian of her beloved father. Sayyidah Fatimah is the one who cared for her father the most after the passing of her beloved mother, Sayyidah Khadijah, and Abu Talib in the year 619 CE.

During the Year of Sorrow after the passing of Sayyidah Khadijah, her young daughter said, "I do not know what to say except, 'most certainly it is true that from Allah we come and to Him we shall return.' "

It is reported that she also made the following supplication, "Oh Allah strengthen me as I bear my mother's passing. I do not know whether I should be sad because of her passing, or happy about the news Allah has given her [in regard to her high ranking and status in Paradise]."

Furthermore, the death of Abu Talib stripped the Prophet ﷺ of his tribal protection within Makkah. The Messenger of Allah ﷺ knew full well that after many years in Makkah it was now time for him to make the migration to Madinah. The atmosphere in Makkah was starting to become more hostile day after day because of Abu Talib's death. Abu Jahl became more rebellious, so much so, that he sought the help of the surrounding tribes to attack the Messenger of Allah ﷺ, his family, and companions.

It was around this time that the Messenger of Allah ﷺ is famously known to have said, *"The Quraysh would never dare treat me this way while Abu Talib was alive."*[126]

The one who comforted the Messenger of Allah ﷺ the most during this time of hardship was Sayyidah Fatimah al-Zahrah. She even gained the nickname *Umm Abiha* (the mother of her father) because of the support she provided to him during these times.

This sorrow was added to by the Quraysh continuing to mock the Prophet ﷺ. Hafiz ibn Kathir explained, "After the passing of multiple of the Prophet's ﷺ male children, the Quraysh started laughing at the Prophet ﷺ and they would follow him around Makkah, saying things like, 'You are cut off, you have no male children, your lineage is a joke, etc.' "

When they incessantly pestered the Prophet ﷺ with this nonsense it made Fatimah very upset and thus her father al-Mustafa ﷺ became angry as well. This type of abuse was uncalled for. Their wild behaviour was far from excusable, and Allah ﷻ answered this in a number of verses He revealed against the leaders of the Quraysh.

The Prophet ﷺ said, as related by both Ali ibn Abi Talib and Muhammad ibn Ali (al-Hanifiyyah), *"Fatimah is a part of me. Therefore, whoever angers her has angered me."*[127]

After some time, the Prophet ﷺ was given glad tidings of abundance – Allah ﷻ revealed the Surah of al-Kawthar, saying:

> ***Indeed, We have given you the Kawthar.***
> ***So make sure you pray unto your Lord! And offer sacrifice.***
> ***Truly, your enemy (the leaders of the Quraysh) shall be the one cut off (in his progeny).*** (Q.108:1-3)[128]

In addition to this the Messenger of Allah ﷺ said, *"All the children of a mother are attributed to their fatherly relation except the sons of Fatimah."*[129]

Allah ﷻ comforted the Prophet ﷺ by pointing out to him that the abundant good – al-Kawthar – was pointing to the abundant offspring which the Prophet ﷺ would have through his daughter Sayyidah Fatimah. This indeed came into fruition with the births of Imams al-Hasan and al-Husayn and their offspring.[130]

This is not the only meaning of the verse of course and Allah ﷻ knows best.

In regard to the greatness of his beloved daughter, the Prophet ﷺ said, *"Truly, Fatimah has protected her honor and purity in such a way that Allah has protected her and her children from the fire."*[131]

Sayyidah Fatimah al-Zahrah herself narrates from her father, al-Mustafa ﷺ, who said, *"The lineage of every mother's children is attributed to their father except for Fatimah's children. So I (the Prophet ﷺ) am their guardian and I am their lineage."*[132]

Much more can be said, yet brevity is sunnah and with Allah ﷻ is the success.

Chapter 17:

The Mine of Madinah

We now enter the Mine of Madinah. After hearing the news of an imminent attack on his life, the Messenger of Allah ﷺ left Makkah in the dark of the night with Sayyiduna Abu Bakr al-Siddique, heading to Madinah al-Munawwarah. This journey is known as the *hijrah,* or the migration. The Qurayshi leaders tried their hardest to track down the two, yet Allah ﷻ protected them and allowed their safe arrival into Madinah al-Munawwarah.

Shortly after the Prophet ﷺ migrated to Madinah, Sayyiduna Ali, after returning the property belonging to Quraysh that had been entrusted to the Prophet ﷺ, was responsible for accompanying the three Fatimahs to the city of Madinah. They were Fatimah al-Zahrah, the daughter of the Messenger of Allah ﷺ, Sayyiduna Ali's own mother, Fatimah bint Asad and the other Fatimah being the daughter of Hamzah ibn Abd al-Muttalib. On their way to Madinah, they were chased by the Quraysh. However, Allah ﷻ made it that they were able to evade them and they all arrived safely at Quba and then travelled to Madinah.

On the night of the *hijrah* of the Prophet ﷺ and Sayyiduna Abu Bakr al-Siddique, Sayyiduna Ali ibn Abi Talib risked his life to protect the Messenger of Allah ﷺ so he could escape persecution in Makkah. This night is known as Laylatun Nabit in the year 622 CE. Now when Allah ﷻ willed for the Messenger of Allah ﷺ to make the migration to Madinah, that same night the Quraysh met at Dar al-Nadwa and plotted to kill the Messenger of Allah ﷺ. Allah ﷻ says about the Quraysh, ***"They want to extinguish the light of Allah with their mouths, but Allah will perfect His light, although those without faith dislike it."*** (Q.61:8)

The tribes of the Quraysh surrounded the house of our beloved Prophet ﷺ, and the Messenger of Allah ﷺ knowing this would happen, told Ali, *"Sleep in my bed; wrap yourself in this green cloak of mine and sleep in it, and no harm will befall you from them."* Allah ﷻ also revealed a verse in regard to Sayyiduna Ali, ***"And among men is he [Ali ibn Abi Talib] who sells himself to seek the pleasure of Allah."*** (Q.2:207) Abdullah ibn Abbas said in relation to the above verse, "Ali sold himself [purchased paradise] that night [Laylatun Nabit], when he put on the cloak of the Prophet ﷺ and then slept in his place."

Imam al-Tabari notes, "This showed Ali's willingness to sacrifice his life for the Prophet ﷺ." Imam ibn Hisham noted, "When the Messenger of Allah ﷺ made the intention to make the migration from Makkah to Madinah, men from each major tribe of Quraysh were outside the house of the Messenger of Allah ﷺ, so he recited a verse from Surah Ya-Sin, ***'And We have put a barrier before them, and a barrier behind them, and We have covered them up, so that they cannot see.'"*** (Q.36:9)

Being shielded by Allah ﷻ, they were able to migrate and they ended up being chased by the Quraysh. The Messenger of Allah ﷺ and Abu Bakr al-Siddique hid in the cave of Thawr for three days until the search for them died down. The Quraysh searched for them so hard until they traced their trail right up to the mouth of a cave. At this point they saw a spider's web covering the entrance to the cave and thus thought the cave was uninhabited. Imam al-Bukhari notes in regard to this, "Sayyiduna Abu Bakr said, 'If any of them looks down at their feet, they will see us.' " The Prophet ﷺ replied to him, thus calming him down, saying, *"What do you think about two companions, of whom Allah is the third?"* After three days, the two companions found a guide and proceeded to Madinah. This is how the *seerah* explains the migration of the beloved Messenger of Allah ﷺ, Ali ibn Abi Talib and Sayyiduna Abu Bakr. Allah ﷻ revealed a verse in regard to this event as well. He says, ***"If you [people of Quraysh] do not aid him, Allah has already aided him when those who disbelieved had driven him out [of Makkah] as one of the two, when they [i.e. the Messenger of Allah ﷺ and Abu Bakr] were in the cave and he said to his companion 'Do not grieve [O Abu Bakr!]; indeed Allah is with us.' And Allah sent down His tranquility, upon him and supported him with soldiers [i.e. angels] you did not see and made the word of those who disbelieved the lowest, while the word of Allah – that is the highest. And Allah is Exalted in Might and Wise."*** (Q.9:40)

Sayyiduna Ali had to delay his migration to Madinah because he was entrusted to return all of the property belonging to the Quraysh that was in the possession of the Messenger of Allah ﷺ, thereby honouring his commitment to them, despite their aggression towards him.

Now, while our beloved Messenger of Allah ﷺ made the migration with Sayyiduna Abu Bakr al-Siddique, one must remember that Sayyiduna Ali not only slept in the bed of the Messenger of Allah ﷺ, he also stayed behind to return all of the belongings left in the trust of the Messenger of Allah ﷺ by the Quraysh. Allah ﷻ speaks of this in the Qur'an when He says, ***"Truly! Allah commands that you should render back the trusts to those to whom they are due; and that when you judge between men, you judge with justice. Truly, how excellent is the teaching which He gives you! Truly, Allah is the One who Hears and Sees Everything."*** (Q.4:58)

Allah ﷻ also says, ***"We know indeed the grief which their words cause you [Oh Messenger of Allah!]: it is not you that they deny, but it is the verses [the Qur'an] of Allah that the oppressors deny."*** (Q.6:33)

This verse demonstrates that all of the Quraysh knew the Messenger of Allah ﷺ to be al-Amin, the trustworthy one, even before the advent of the message of Islam. They knew well to entrust their wealth with such an honest person. May Allah ﷻ bless our beloved Prophet ﷺ for being such an example of trustworthiness in life.

With this event, we see the the bravery of Sayyiduna Ali, as well as his willingness to put himself right in the line of fire. Throughout the whole ordeal, Sayyiduna Ali was calm and collected, and was one of the last Muslims to make the *hijrah* to the illuminated city of Madinah. This is amazing indeed.

It is as if Ali was implementing the verse of the Qur'an, ***"The Prophet is closer to the believers than their own selves, and his wives are their mothers."*** (Q.33:6)

Finally, Sayyiduna Ali and Sayyidah Fatimah met up with the Messenger of Allah ﷺ, who waited for them in Quba[133] before going to Madinah. Sayyidah Fatimah al-Zahrah was overflowing with joy upon seeing her father, after having worried about him so much during his journey.

These were beautiful times as Sayyiduna Ali (and Sayyidah Fatimah), who had left Makkah by foot three days after the Prophet ﷺ, had also arrived. The Prophet ﷺ, his companions from Makkah, and the helpers [*ansar*] of Quba led him to Madinah, where they had been eagerly anticipating his arrival. It is at Quba that the prayer direction was later changed, as is narrated on the authority of Abdullah ibn Umar who said, "While some people were offering Fajr prayer at Quba Masjid, someone came to them and said, 'Specific verses of the Qur'an have been revealed to the Messenger of Allah ﷺ tonight, and he has been ordered to face the Ka'bah (of Makkah) so you too, should turn your faces towards it.' Their faces were then towards Sham (Jerusalem), so they turned towards the Qibla (i.e. Ka'bah of Makkah)."[134]

Anas ibn Malik, a close companion of the Prophet ﷺ said, "When it was the day in which the Messenger of Allah ﷺ entered Madinah, everything became illuminated by him. When it was the day in which the Messenger of Allah ﷺ left this world, everything became dark. We had not yet dusted the blessed earth [of his burial] from our hands, but our hearts rejected [the change]."[135]

Imam al-Bukhari and Muslim also relate, "Every house in Madinah wished that the Prophet ﷺ would stay with them, and some tried to lead his camel to their home. The Prophet ﷺ stopped them and said, *'Leave her, for she is under (Divine) Command.'* It passed many houses until it came to a halt and knelt at the land of Banu Najjar. The Prophet ﷺ did not descend until the camel had risen and gone on a little, then it turned and went back to its original place and knelt again. Upon that, the Prophet ﷺ descended from it. He was pleased with its choice, for Banu Najjar were his maternal uncles, and he also desired to honour them. When individuals from the family were soliciting him to enter their houses, a certain Abu Ayyub stepped forward to his saddle and took it into his house. The Prophet ﷺ said, *'A man goes with his saddle.'* "[136] It is recorded that the Messenger of Allah ﷺ chose to stay with the *sahabi* Abu Ayyub al-Ansari.[137]

While in Madinah, Sayyidah Fatimah shared the struggle of her father and the Muslims. When the Quraysh would wage war against the Muslims she would do her part to help out and tend to the wounded and injured. In fact, it is narrated that at Uhud the face of the Prophet ﷺ was wounded; one of his front teeth was broken and the helmet over his head was smashed. Sayyidah Fatimah attended to him and washed off the blood while Ali held the water. When Sayyidah Fatimah saw that the bleeding was increasing, she burnt a mat (of date-palm leaves) till it turned into ashes, which she put over the wound and thus stopped the Messenger of Allah ﷺ bleeding.[138]

Sayyidah Fatimah also shared in their poverty. While we will mention below her sacrifices for the poor and needy, the following narration shows how she put others above herself, "Once Sayyidah Fatimah took the Prophet ﷺ a piece of bread. He asked, 'What's this, Fatimah?' She replied, 'It is a loaf I baked and I could not feel at ease until I brought it to you.' The Prophet ﷺ said, ' Indeed, it is the first food to enter your father's mouth for three days.' "[139]

Much more can be said, yet brevity is sunnah and with Allah ﷻ is the success.

Chapter 18:

The Mine of Marriage

We now enter the Mine of Marriage and will start by researching the benefits of married life and the blessing of bearing children.

To start, Allah ﷻ says, ***"And marry those among you who are single."*** (Q.24:32)

The most exemplary marriage to take as our model is of course the marriage of the Prophet Muhammad ﷺ and his beloved wife Sayyidah Khadijah bint Khuwaylid. The marriage of Sayyiduna Ali ibn Abi Talib and Sayyidah Fatimah in turn was a mirror of this Prophetic union.

The Messenger of Allah ﷺ told Sayyiduna Ali, *"Three things should not be delayed in Islam: 1) the prayer when it's time has come 2) the funeral prayer [Salat al-Janaza] when the deceased is prepared and (the people are) present and 3) the marriage of an unwed woman when her match is found."*[140]

The Prophet Muhammad ﷺ also said, *"Four things if granted to any person, he is granted the best of the world and the afterlife: 1) a thankful heart,*

2) a tongue that mentions Allah, 3) a body that patiently endures misfortune, and 4) a wife that does not seek his betrayal or his money."[141]

Implementing the good of the above, O Allah! we ask you, ***"Our Lord! Bestow on us from our wives and our offspring, those who will be the comfort of our eyes, and make us leaders among the righteous."*** (Q.25:74) All while following the footsteps of Your beloved Messenger ﷺ, who said, *"The best of you is he who is the best to his family, and I am the best to my family."*[142]

Sayyiduna Ali ibn Abi Talib said, "Goodness is not in your wealth and offspring being plentiful; true goodness is when your [good] deeds are plenty and you have great understanding and forbearance, and when you compete to worship your Lord. If you do good you praise Allah and thank Him, and if you sin you beg the forgiveness of Allah. There is no good in this life except with two types of men: A man who sins but then corrects himself through repentance, and a man who strives and hastens to get the good of the hereafter."[143]

Marriage is something that must be yearned for, in fact it is a Prophetic sunnah. It was narrated from Sayyidah Aisha al-Siddiqah, that the Messenger of Allah ﷺ said, *"Marriage is part of my sunnah [Prophetic way], and whoever does not follow my sunnah has nothing to do with me. Get married, for I will boast of your great numbers before the nations. Whoever has the means, let him get married, and whoever does not, then he should fast for it will diminish his desire."*[144]

All praise is due to Allah, ﷻ by fulfilling the vow of marriage we have the opportunity to fulfill a Prophetic sunnah, as Allah ﷻ says, ***"And, indeed, We sent Messengers before you, and We gave them wives and children…"*** (Q.13:38)

The Messenger of Allah ﷺ said, *"By Allah, I am more submissive to Allah and more afraid of Him than you; yet I fast and break my fast, I lay down at night and I also marry women. So he who does not follow my tradition in religion, is not from me [not one of my followers]."*[145]

The Messenger of Allah ﷺ said, *"Marriage is of my sunnah; whoever likes my natural disposition [fitra], let him follow my sunnah,"* and, *"What I like the most from your world are three things: 1) women*[146]*, 2) scent, and 3) prayer, which is the coolness of my eye. [meaning the prayer/salat]."*[147][148]

An authentic saying of the Prophet Muhammad ﷺ reads, *"A woman is married for four reasons: 1) her property, 2) her status, 3) her beauty, and 4) her religion; so it is best to choose according to (her) religion."*[149]

The same holds true when looking for a husband, as the Messenger of Allah ﷺ said, *"When someone with whose religion and character you are satisfied asks to marry your daughter, comply with his request. If you do not do so, there will be corruption and great evil on earth."*[150]

And who is better for one another than the Prophet Muhammad ﷺ and his beloved wife Khadijah? Likewise, the same is said for Sayyidah Fatimah al-Zahrah and Sayyiduna Ali as they were the shining lights and mirrors of the Prophetic household.

The Blessings of Marriage

There are many verses of the Qur'an that speak about the benefits of marriage. Let's look at some of these jewels:

"Among His proofs is that He created for you spouses from among yourselves, in order to have tranquility and contentment with each other, and He placed in your hearts love and care towards your spouses. In this, there are sufficient proofs for people who think." (Q.30:21)

"It is He who created the human being from water, then invested him with ties of blood and marriage, and your Lord is all-powerful." (Q.25:54)

"The believers, men and women, are protectors, of one another," (Q.9:71) and, ***"He made mates for you from among yourselves, multiplying you thereby."*** (Q.42:11)

"Your wives are a garment for you, and you are a garment for them." (Q.2:187)

Allah says, ***"O you who believe! Make not unlawful the good things which Allah has made lawful for you, but commit no transgression."*** (Q.5:87)

"And good women are for good men and good men are for good women." (Q.24:26)

"Never will I allow to be lost the work of any of you, be he male or female." (Q.3:195)

"And they (your wives) have made with you a firm covenant." (Q.4:21)

"He it is Who created you from a single being, and of the same kind did He make his mate that he might incline to her." (Q.7:189)

"O you who believe, let not your wealth nor your children divert you from the remembrance of Allah. And whoever does that are indeed those in loss." (Q.63:9)

From the sunnah there are many examples as well. For example, the companion Anas ibn Malik narrated that the Prophet ﷺ said, *"When a man gets married, he gets one half of the religion. Thus, he should fear Allah in regard to the other half."*[151]

O Allah! ***"O my Lord! Truly I am in need of whatever good You bestow on me."*** (Q.28:24)

The Messenger of Allah ﷺ said, *"All of you are shepherds and all of you will be asked about your wards. The man is responsible for his household and will be asked about his responsibilities. The wife will be asked about the house of her husband and her responsibilities."*[152]

"O you who believe! Protect yourselves and your families against a fire (Hell) whose fuel is men and stones, over which are (appointed) angels, stern and severe, and who disobey not the commands they receive from Allah, but do that which they are commanded." (Q.66:6) Sayyiduna Ali ibn Abi Talib said concerning this verse, "This verse calls for the head of the household to discipline and teach the family." Abdullah ibn Abbas said it means to "stay obedient to Allah, stay away from disobeying Allah and command your families to remember Allah, and He will save you from the Fire".[153]

It was narrated from Jabir that the Messenger of Allah ﷺ said in his farewell sermon, *"Fear Allah concerning women! Truly, you have taken them on the security of Allah, and intercourse with them has been made lawful unto you by words of Allah. You too have rights over them, and that they should not allow anyone to sit on your bed or enter your house whom you do not like. But if they do that, you can chastise them but not severely. Their rights upon you are that you should provide them with food and clothing in a fitting manner."*[154]

Always remember Allah ﷻ says, ***"And they (women) have rights (over their husbands) similar (to those of their husbands) over them to what is reasonable, but men have a degree (of responsibility) over them."*** (Q.2:228)

Allah ﷻ says, ***"Men are the protectors and maintainers of women, because Allah has made one of them to excel the other, and because they spend (to support them) from their means."*** (Q.4:34)

One of the explanations of the above verse is, they must spiritually, mentally and financially support the wife.[155]

Abdullah ibn Abbas said, "They have the right to good companionship and kind and reasonable treatment from their husbands just as they are obliged to obey the commands of their husbands."[156]

Imam al-Tabari noted, "And it was said that they have the right that their husbands should not harm them, and their husbands have a similar right over them."[157]

The Christians have a similar belief found in the Book of Genesis which reads, "Therefore, a man leaves his father and his mother and cleaves to his wife, and they become one flesh."

Imam al-Daylami, said, "The act of getting married is the greatest pilgrimage [*Hajj al-Akbar*]. Whosoever spends his money for Hajj on his marriage, Allah will also reward him with the virtue for Hajj. Marriage is like the fortress of an army."[158]

Dr. Muhammad Tahir al-Qadiri mentioned the marriage of Ali and Fatimah in the most beautiful way when he said, "For years I wondered why Imam Ali al-Murtadha was born inside the Ka'bah (the House of Allah ﷻ). I did a lot of research (without finding any answers). The answer came to me the day I reflected on the day of Shah-e-Mardan's wedding. It was intended by Allah ﷻ that if the bride (Sayyidah Fatimah al-Zahrah) was to be from the House of al-Mustafa ﷺ then the groom (Ali ibn Abi Talib) had to be from the House of Allah ﷻ."[159]

The Husband of Sayyidah Fatimah al-Zahrah: Sayyiduna Ali ibn Abi Talib

Anas ibn Malik narrates that the Prophet Muhammad ﷺ said, *"Every prophet has an example, and my example is in the person of Ali."*[160]

Jabir ibn Abdullah said, "I heard Ali recite the following verses as the Messenger of Allah ﷺ listened:

I am Muhammad's brother. My Lineage is incontestable:
I was brought up with him; his two grandsons are my sons;
My grandfather and his grandfather are one;
and Fatimah is my wife. All True.
I believed in him when the world
Was in the throes of error, polytheism, and adversity.
All praise and gratitude are due to God. He has no partner.
He is kind to his servants, and eternal, without end.

'You have spoken true, Ali', the Prophet ﷺ responded."[161]

An example of the good demeanor of Sayyiduna Ali can be found in the following saying, "Be like the bee – when it eats, it eats what is good and when it secretes, it secretes what is good, and when it sits on a twig it does not break it."[162]

This good nature of course won the heart of the Prophet Muhammad ﷺ and he told him, *"O Ali! before you, other men had come to get the hand of Fatimah and whenever I informed Fatimah of this matter, she would not show her approval. So as of now, let me inform her of your proposal and this conversation."*

When the Prophet ﷺ told her of what Ali had said, he then asked Fatimah if she would be interested in marrying Ali. She did not frown or look concerned and she remained silent, which indicated her acceptance.

After his beloved daughter accepted the proposal of Sayyiduna Ali, the Prophet ﷺ exclaimed in joy, *"Allahu Akbar! Her silence is the proof of her agreement."*

The Prophet ﷺ at that moment was the happiest father in the world as he knew the good character of Ali, as he himself was the one who raised Ali. In fact, Sayyiduna Ali learned all of his good traits from the Prophet Muhammad ﷺ and this is why the Prophet ﷺ said, *"The one who wants to live my life and die my death will attach himself to Ali."*[163]

This distinction is like a gift to Ali ibn Abi Talib for being the spiritual brother of the Prophet ﷺ. The proof for this is in the narration of Abdullah ibn Umar where he narrated, "The Messenger of Allah ﷺ made bonds of brotherhood among his Companions. So Ali came to him (literally) crying and saying, 'O Messenger of Allah ﷺ! You have made a bond of brotherhood among your Companions, but you have not made a bond of brotherhood with me and anyone else.' So the Messenger of Allah ﷺ said to him, *'I am your brother, in this life and the next.'* "[164]

Truly, Ali is a man to be obeyed and emulated, a true man of *futuwwa* (spiritual chivalry).

The Messenger of Allah ﷺ also said in relation to this, *"Whoever obeys Ali, obeys me, whoever obeys me, obeys Allah, whoever disobeys Ali disobeys me, whoever disobeys me, disobeys Allah."*[165]

Ali is continually connected to the Prophet ﷺ in many sayings. For example, *"O Ali! Whoever separates from me, he separates from Allah; and whoever separates from you, he separates from me."*[166] and, *"We were created from the same tree, I and Ali."*[167] as well as, *"Ali is from me and I am from Ali."*[168] and, *"You are of me and I am of you."*[169]

Imam Ibn Hajar Asqalani explained, "That is, in lineage, relationship by marriage, in seniority (in Islam), in love and in other ways."[170]

The Messenger of Allah ﷺ also said, *"The title of the believer's book is love for Ali."*[171]

Imam al-Bayhaqi also relates two beautiful jewels of hadith where it is said, *"The one who wants to see Adam's knowledge, Nuh's piety, Ibrahim's forbearance, and Musa's worship, then let him look at Ali ibn Abi Talib,"* and, *"The one who wants to see Adam's knowledge, Nuh's intelligence, Yahya ibn Zakariyya's abstinence, and Musa ibn Imran's power, then let him look at Ali ibn Abi Talib."*[172]

Sayyiduna Ali's spiritual mastery is so famous within the circles of spirituality that one of the sultans of the path, Imam Junayd al-Baghdadi said, "Ali is the Chief Sultan of all of the friends of Allah and it is based upon his principles and practices of spirituality that we rely upon."[173]

Sayyiduna Ali's example as someone who would go through many trials himself is well-known. The Messenger of Allah ﷺ knew this and thus he is known to have said, as is narrated on the authority of Abu Hurayrah, " *'Out of everyone, I am the closest to Isa, the son of Maryam, among all of mankind, concerning this worldly life and the hereafter.'* The Companions said, O Messenger of Allah! ﷺ in what way do you mean? Thereupon the Messenger of Allah ﷺ said, *'The Prophets are brothers in faith, having different mothers. However, their religion is one and there is no Prophet between myself and Isa.'* "[174]

Allah ﷻ says concerning this, ***"And when the son of Maryam is cited as an example, behold, people make mockery of it."*** (Q.43:57)

Now, as we look at the above, remember that Sayyidah Fatimah has her own connection to Sayyidah Maryam, the mother of Isa. We should also note that it is very significant that Ali tells us, "The Messenger of Allah ﷺ called me and told me, *'You are similar to Isa the son of Maryam,*[175] *the Jews hated him to the point that they slandered his mother, and the Christians loved him to the point that they put him in a position that is not suited for him.'* "[176]

The spiritual companionship between the Messenger of Allah ﷺ and Sayyiduna Ali was beyond imagination, yet to give you an example the Prophet ﷺ said, *"O Ali! I wish to achieve every such thing for you that I desire to acquire myself and I want to keep you away from all those things which I abhor."*[177]

This intense love for the Messenger of Allah ﷺ is necessary for every believer, as the Messenger of Allah ﷺ once said, *"None of you will truly have faith until he loves me more than his father, his children and all mankind."*[178]

Sayyiduna Ali ibn Abi Talib was asked, "How was your love for the Messenger of Allah ﷺ?" He replied, "By Allah, we loved him more than our wealth, our sons, our fathers and our mothers, and more than cold water in a time of great thirst."[179]

Allah ﷻ also commands the Messenger of Allah ﷺ, ***"Tell the***

people! If you love Allah then you should follow me. Only then will Allah love you and forgive your sins. And Allah is All-Forgiving, All-Merciful," (Q.3:31) and, ***"All who obey Allah and the Messenger are in the company of those on whom is the Grace of Allah, from among the Prophets, the sincere ones, the witnesses, and the Righteous: Ah! what a beautiful fellowship."*** (Q.4:69)

Sayyiduna Ali most certainly lived his life according to the following verse, ***"O You who believe! Obey Allah, and obey the Messenger and those who are given authority among you; and then if you ever dispute about something, then refer it to Allah and the Messenger,"*** (Q.4:59) and, ***"He who obeys the Messenger has obeyed Allah."*** (Q.4:80)

This is as the great *mufassir* of the Qur'an, Imam Sahl al-Tustari said, "Whoever does not think the Messenger is his master in all states or think that he is under the dominion of the Prophet ﷺ does not taste the sweetness of his sunnah because the Prophet, may Allah bless him and grant him peace, said, *'None of you will believe until I am dearer to him than himself.'* "[180]

Sayyiduna Ali himself said, "I was still a young child when the Prophet ﷺ took me into his custody. I would stick by him at all times and he used to feed me, and because of this companionship, when I grew a little older, he saw that I never told a lie, nor have I ever tried to deceive people. In regard to me, the Prophet ﷺ was like a guiding star and I used to follow his actions and deeds very carefully. I was attached to him like a newborn camel attached to its mother. He always taught me about and emphasized the importance of high moral values, and he advised me to make sure that I follow them [these moral values]. There was a time every year, that he would spend a few days at the grotto of mount Hira and I used to go with him. I was his only companion then and none else could meet him at Hira. It was there that I used to see the light of revelation, and used to smell the fragrance of prophethood. Once the Prophet ﷺ told me, *'Ali! You have attained a very eminent place. This is because you see what I see and you hear what I hear.'* "[181]

Imam al-Tabari and many other scholars of Qur'an and hadith narrate that the Prophet ﷺ said, " *'Shall I guide you to something which, if you grasp it after me, you will never go astray?'* The Companions [*sahaba*] of the Messenger of Allah ﷺ submitted, 'Yes, O Messenger of Allah ﷺ!' He ﷺ pointed and said, *'It is Ali'* "[182]

His Bravery

Sayyiduna Ali is the hero of the Battle of Badr (624 CE). Sayyiduna Ali said, "When the fighting grew intense on the day of [the Battle of] Badr we sought shelter by drawing closer to the Messenger of Allah ﷺ who was one of the strongest of men, and nobody was closer [in proximity] to the enemy than him."[183]

In the book *Kitab Al-Maghazi* it is related, "It was in this Battle of Badr that Sayyiduna Ali first distinguished himself as a warrior. This happened because he defeated the Umayyad champion, Walid ibn Utba, as well as twenty other Makkan soldiers."[184]

Qatada said, "Ali ibn Abi Talib, was the standard-bearer of the Prophet ﷺ in the Battle of Badr."[185]

Imam Abu Dawud reports Ali ibn Abi Talib as saying, "(At the battle of Badr) Utbah ibn Rabi'ah came forward followed by his son and his brother and cried out, 'Who will be engaged in single combat?' Some young men of the Helpers responded to his call. He asked, 'Who are you?' They told him. He said, 'We do not want you; we, in fact, want only our cousins.' The Prophet ﷺ said, *'Get up Hamzah, get up Ali, get up Ubaydah ibn al-Harith.'* Hamzah went forward to Utbah, I went forward to Shaybah; and after two blows had been exchanged between Ubaydah and al-Walid, they wounded one another severely; so we turned against al-Walid and killed him, and we carried Ubaydah away."[186]

It is during this famous battle that the Messenger of Allah ﷺ gave his sword, Dhul-Fiqar, to Ali after the battle was finished.

At the battle of Uhud Sayyiduna Ali, his uncle Sayyiduna Hamzah and Abu Dujana were counted among the heroes. This is the battle where Sayyiduna Ali distinguished himself as a true champion of Allah ﷻ. He fought fearlessly and ran through the standard bearer of the Quraysh, a man by the name of Talha ibn Abu Talha. The standard was immediately raised by another man named Uthman ibn Abu Talha. And when Uthman fell at the hands of Hamzah, it was raised again by Abu Sa'd ibn Abu Talha. He shouted at the Muslims, "Do you pretend that your martyrs are in paradise and ours in hell? By God, you lie! If anyone of you truly believes such a story, let him come forward and fight with me." This challenge attracted Sayyiduna Ali, who killed him on the spot.[187]

During the battle a false rumor was spread about the Messenger of Allah ﷺ being killed. This confused the generals and soldiers of the Muslims because the Quraysh were now shouting, "we have killed Muhammad, we have killed Muhammad!" Hearing this, many *sahaba* fled, with only a few from the *sahaba* staying to protect the Messenger of Allah ﷺ, Sayyiduna Ali of course being one of them.

Allah ﷻ speaks about this in the Qur'an, ***"When you ran off precipitately and did not wait for anyone, and the Messenger was calling you from your rear."*** (Q.3:153)

Abdullah ibn Abbas said, "Among the virtues of Ali is that he is one who stayed with the Messenger of Allah ﷺ at all times, during the Battle on the day of al-Mihras [the Battle of Uhud]."[188]

The Messenger of Allah ﷺ said concerning Sayyiduna Ali's valor in the Battle of Uhud, *"There is no sword but Dhul-Fiqar, and there is no young warrior who can compare to Ali."*[189]

Sahl narrated that he was asked about the wound of the Prophet ﷺ on the day of the battle of Uhud. He said, "The face of the Prophet ﷺ was wounded and one of his front teeth was broken and the helmet over his head was smashed. Fatimah washed off the blood while Ali held the water. When she saw that the bleeding was increasing, she burnt a mat (of date-palm leaves) till it turned into ashes which she put over the wound and thus the bleeding ceased."[190]

Sahl ibn Sa'd narrated, "On the day (of the battle) of Khaybar the Prophet ﷺ said, *'Tomorrow I will give the flag to somebody who will be given victory (by Allah) and who loves Allah and His Messenger and is loved by Allah and His Messenger.'* So, the people wondered all that night as to who would receive the flag, and in the morning everyone hoped that he would be that person. The Messenger of Allah ﷺ asked, *'Where is Ali?'* He was told that Ali was suffering from eye-trouble, so he applied saliva to his eyes and invoked Allah to cure him. He at once got cured as if he had no ailment. The Prophet ﷺ gave him the flag. Ali said, 'Should I struggle against them till they become like us?' The Prophet ﷺ said, *'Go to them patiently and calmly till you enter the land. Then, invite them to Islam, and inform them what is enjoined upon them, for, by Allah, if Allah gives guidance to somebody through you, it is better for you than possessing red camels.'*"[191]

Abu Rafi said, "We went out with Ali ibn Abi Talib, when the Messenger of Allah ﷺ dispatched him with his flag against Khaybar. When he reached near the fortress, its people came out against him and he engaged them in battle. One of the Jews struck at him and knocked his shield from his hands. Ali then grasped the door of the fortress, which was made from iron, and used it as a shield. It remained in his hand as he fought the Jews until Allah conquered the fortress by his hands. After Ali had conquered Khaybar he threw the door a distance of eighty feet behind his back."[192]

Muhammad ibn Ishaq says that this is because, "Marhab had hit the shield of Sayyiduna Ali and knocked it out of his hands, thus he snatched the door from its hinges."

Imam Suyuti said it took 40 men to move it, while Imam al-Bayhaqi related that after Ali tossed the door, it took 70 men to return the door to its hinges. This incident was seen as a miracle from Allah ﷻ and from this point, people really started revering Sayyiduna Ali ibn Abi Talib.

Shaykh Ahmad ibn Hajr al-Haytami relates that Ali said, "I did not snatch the door of Khaybar from its place by bodily power, but by power from the Divine."[193] The narrator goes on to say, "at this time Sayyiduna Ali struck Marhab straight in the head and he died from it, thus both the victory and capture of Khaybar was due to him."

In the *Mathnawi* of Mawlana Rumi, we find a beautiful narration of an incident that took place between Ali and a warrior which has been traditionally considered to have taken place at the Battle of Khaybar. Ali had gotten the better of this warrior and was hovering over him about to kill him, whereupon the infidel warrior spat upon the face of Ali. Quite to the warrior's surprise, Ali sheathed his sword, sparing his life. The narration is as follows:

> Learn how to act sincerely from Ali: know that the
> Lion of God (Ali) was purged of (all) deceit.

> In fighting against the infidels he got the upper hand of (vanquished) a certain knight, and quickly drew a sword and made haste (to slay him).
>
> He spat on the face of Ali, the pride of every prophet and every saint;
>
> He spat on the countenance before which the face of the moon bows low in the place of worship.
>
> Ali at once threw his sword away and relaxed (his efforts) in fighting him.
>
> That champion was astounded by this act and by his showing forgiveness and mercy without occasion.
>
> *He* said, "You lifted your keen sword against me: why have you flung it aside and spared me?
>
> What did you see that was better than combat with me, so that you have become slack in hunting me down?"

Sayyiduna Ali responded to the man:

> He said, "I am wielding the sword for God's sake, I am the servant of God, I am not under the command of the body.
>
> I am the Lion of God, I am not the lion of passion: my deed bears witness to my religion.
>
> In war I am (manifesting the truth of) thou didst not throw when thou threwest: I am (but) as the sword, and the wielder is the (Divine) Sun.
>
> I have removed the baggage of self out of the way,
> I have deemed (what is) other than God to be nonexistence.
>
> I am a shadow, the Sun is my lord; I am the chamberlain,
> I am not the curtain (which prevents approach) to Him.

I am filled with the pearls of union, like a (jewelled) sword: in battle I make (men) living, not slain.

Blood does not cover the sheen of my sword: how should the wind sweep away my clouds?

I am not a straw, I am a mountain of forbearance and patience and justice: how should the fierce wind carry off the mountain?"[194]

The Courtship of Sayyidah Fatimah and Sayyiduna Ali[195]

Allah ﷻ says, ***"Truly, those who believe and work deeds of righteousness, the Most-Gracious will bestow upon them love."*** (Q.19:96)

"They hope for a commerce that will never be unprofitable." (Q.35:29)

Sayyiduna Ali ibn Abi Talib also said, "My longing is not stirred save by His wind; my captain is naught but love of the One."[196]

Shaykh Abd al-Qadir Al-Jilani said in regard to this:

Lovers have eyes in their hearts.
They see, while others are staring blind.
Such wings they have, not of flesh and blood.
They fly towards angels, their Lord to find.[197]

When the time came for Sayyidah Fatimah al-Zahrah to be married, many prominent members of the companions of the Messenger of Allah ﷺ were beginning to sense that Sayyiduna Ali ibn Abi Talib was decreed to marry Sayyidah Fatimah, and so they were approaching him daily saying things like, "Why do you not ask for the hand of the daughter of the Messenger of Allah ﷺ?" Sayyiduna Abu Bakr al-Siddique was among the first of those eager to see their marriage union take place. He, himself being a close friend and brother of the Messenger of Allah ﷺ, had asked for Fatimah's hand in marriage.

Seeing that everyone was being turned down, and with the encouragement of Abu Bakr al-Siddique and other companions (*sahaba*), Sayyiduna Ali finally plucked up the courage to directly ask the Messenger of Allah ﷺ for his daughter's hand in marriage. One can only imagine how much Sayyiduna Ali was shaking!

He walked up to the Messenger of Allah ﷺ and seeing his condition, the Messenger of Allah ﷺ said, *"What brings you here? Do you need something?"*

Sayyiduna Ali said, "I was too shy to say anything, so he told me, *'Unless I am mistaken, I thought you were here to ask for the hand of Fatimah in marriage?'* I said, 'well, yes.' The Prophet ﷺ said, *'Well, can you meet the condition of the dowry and give her something?'* "

Sayyiduna Ali lived a very simple life and so responded, "I do not have a thing to give her for a dowry." The Prophet ﷺ said, *"What about the armor I gave you?"* Sayyiduna Ali responded, "Yes! I do have that." The Prophet ﷺ said, *"Then go get it and you can use this as the dowry."* Ali explains, "I sold this armor and this was the dowry for Fatimah the daughter of the Messenger of Allah ﷺ."[198]

Therefore Sayyiduna Ali became her sanctuary just as Sayyiduna Ibrahim al-Khalil said, 'My Lord, make this land (Makkah) a sanctuary.'

Ali ibn Abi Talib narrated that when Allah ﷻ took the Covenant, He recorded it in writing and fed it to the Black Stone, and this is the meaning of the saying of those who touch the Black Stone during the circumambulation of the Ancient House, "O God! This is believing in You, fulfilling our pledge to You, and declaring the truth of Your record."[199]

Aisha al-Siddiqah said, "(I declare) by Allah that I have not seen anyone more beloved to the Messenger of Allah ﷺ than Ali, nor a woman on earth more beloved to him than his wife (Ali's wife, Fatimah)."[200]

Sayyidah Fatimah al-Zahrah accepted the proposal of Sayyiduna Ali and her silence was as if she was saying to her father, ***"O my father! Hire him! Truly, the best of men for you to hire is the strong, the trustworthy."*** (Q.28:23-26)

It is so true that *"Nothing is better for those in love than marriage"*.[201]

The Prophet Muhammad ﷺ himself was extremely honoured to have his beloved daughter married to Sayyiduna Ali and this proved to be the best decision ever.

Sayyiduna Ali ibn Abi Talib and Sayyidah Fatimah's marriage shows a love like no other. They are the epitome of what it takes to be a good couple. Their love crosses boundaries and teaches us all to struggle with dignity.

Shaykh al-Akbar, Muhyidin ibn Arabi, says in his *Tanazzulat al-Mawsiliyya*, "All praise is due to Allah who made love a sanctuary towards which the hearts of all men whose spiritual education is complete make their way and He made it a Ka'bah around which the secrets of the chests of men of spiritual refinement revolve."

Allah ﷻ says, ***"Exalted is He who created all pairs – from what the earth grows and from themselves and from that which they do not know."*** (Q.36:36)

The Prophet ﷺ stressed the importance of love and marriage in many prophetic sayings and maxims. For example, Abdullah ibn Abbas reported that the Messenger of Allah ﷺ said, *"Nothing is better for those in love than marriage,"*[202] and *"You should marry the religious woman (otherwise) you will be a loser,"*[203] and of course Sayyidah Fatimah was the most religious and most pious, therefore Sayyiduna Ali implemented this sunnah.

The Celestial Marriage of Sayyiduna Ali ibn Abi Talib and Sayyidah Fatimah al-Zahrah

Abdullah ibn Umar said, "Ali had three qualities, had I one of those, I myself would have loved it more than even possessing red camels: 1) he was married to Fatimah al-Zahrah, 2) he was the holder of the flag of Khaybar and 3) he is the one who acted upon the verse of charity before consultation [*Ayat an-Najwa*]."[204]

Sayyiduna Ali ibn Abi Talib is one of the special, chosen servants of Allah ﷻ and his marriage to the daughter of the Prophet ﷺ was special to say the least. It is said that the celestial wedding ceremony of

Sayyiduna Ali and Sayyidah Fatimah took place in the fourth heaven near the *Bayt al-Ma'mur* (the House constantly attended by the angels). It was a unique event the like of which the universe had never encountered before. Angels from all the heavens gathered in the fourth heaven and erected the Minbar of Honour, which is made of light.

The angels said, "The Omnipotent King, chose the one who was bestowed with special Divine Honour, and the worshipper of His Greatness, for His worshipper, the leader of women and the daughter of the best of prophets. Fatimah the splendid is to be married to Ali the devout."

Anas ibn Malik said, "The marriage took place near the Lotus tree in the seventh heaven, on the night of Ascension. (On that occasion) Allah revealed to the tree: 'Sprinkle all that you bear on them.' So it sprinkled them with gems, jewellery and corals."[205]

Abdullah ibn Masud said, "Allah commanded the Tree of Paradise to bear gems and jewellery; He then ordered it to sprinkle them over the angels. So whoever received more than the others on that day, will be proud of it until the Day of Resurrection."[206]

Imam Jalal al-Din al-Suyuti said, "The Prophet ﷺ was in the Masjid when he said to Ali, *'Here is the Angel Jibreel, Peace be upon him, informing me that Allah gave Fatimah to you in marriage, and made forty thousand angels testify to her marriage. He also revealed to the Tree of Tuba to sprinkle them with gems, rubies, jewellery and embellishments. When it had done this, the Huris rushed to collect these gems, rubies, jewellery, and embellishments to exchange them for gifts until the Day of Resurrection.'* "

The Earthly Wedding of Sayyiduna Ali ibn Abi Talib and Sayyidah Fatimah al-Zahrah

The Prophet ﷺ said to his daughter Fatimah, *"I gave you in marriage to the first one to adhere to Islam from my nation, he is also the most knowledgeable and most patient among them."*[207]

Anas ibn Malik narrated, "After Ali married Fatimah, the Prophet came to her door every morning for forty days and said, *'I am at war with whomever you wage war against, and I am at peace with whomever you keep peace with.'* "[208]

Marriage of course is part of the earthly paradise, for it is what makes one whole and it is truly the best provision. For example, within the *Sahih* of Imam Muslim, the Prophet ﷺ is recorded to have said, *"The whole world is a provision, and the best object of benefit of the world is the pious woman."*[209]

Allah ﷻ loves marriage and taught us a dua to say while married, ***"The believers say: Our Lord, grant us from among our wives and offspring joy to our eyes and make us an example for the righteous."*** (Q.25:74)

Allah ﷻ says, ***"And among His signs is this, that He created for you mates from among yourselves, that you may dwell in peace and tranquility with them, and He has put love and mercy between your hearts: Truly, in that are signs for those who reflect."*** (Q.30:21)

Can we imagine the peace and security Sayyiduna Ali felt with his beloved wife Sayyidah Fatimah?

One day the Prophet ﷺ exited his home and joined his companions with his face beaming with joy. Abdul Rahman ibn Awf, Allah ﷻ be pleased with him, inquired as to the cause of his joy and the Prophet ﷺ said, *"I have received good tidings from my Lord about my brother and the son of my uncle, that Allah has given my daughter Fatimah in marriage to Ali."*[210]

Sayyiduna Ali ibn Abi Talib said, "I came out of the house of the Prophet ﷺ and I was very happy, I met Abu Bakr and Umar on the way. They asked me, 'What has happened that you are so happy?' I said 'The Prophet ﷺ has told me that Allah has married Fatimah to me in the heavens, and now he is going to come out of his home and announce it in public.' Abu Bakr and Umar became extremely happy at this and came to the Masjid with me. The Prophet ﷺ reached there soon, then he told Bilal to gather the migrants from Makkah and the helpers from Madinah, which Bilal did. When all the people had gathered, the Prophet ﷺ sat on the pulpit. After praising Allah, he said, *'O Muslims, Jibreel came to me and informed me that Allah has made the angels witnesses that He has married Fatimah to Ali, and has ordered me to marry Fatimah to Ali and make all of you witnesses on the earth.'"*

In another narration, Sayyiduna Ali ibn Abi Talib narrates that the Messenger of Allah ﷺ said, *"An angel came to me and said: 'Oh*

Muhammad! ﷺ, Allah sends Peace upon you and says, 'I have had your daughter married to Ali ibn Abi Talib in the upper level of the Heavens and now you can also arrange the marriage ceremony of Fatimah with Ali on earth.' "[211]

Upon this news, the Prophet ﷺ told his beloved daughter, Sayyidah Fatimah, *"O Fatimah! Are you not pleased with this, that Allah, the Mighty and Glorious, cast a glance on the dwellers of the earth and selected from them two men, one of them your father and the other your husband?"*[212]

Later in life the Prophet ﷺ would tell her once again, *"Are you not happy that you are the leader of all the women of Paradise and both of your sons are leaders of the youth of Paradise [Jannah]."*[213]

On another occasion the Messenger of Allah ﷺ drew four lines on the ground, then he said, *"Do you know what this is?"* The companions said, "Allah and His messenger know best." The Messenger of Allah ﷺ said, *"The best of the women of paradise are Khadijah bint Khuwaylid, Fatimah bint Muhammad, Asiyah bint Mazahim, and Maryam bint Imran."*[214]

The Dowry, Wedding Feast and Marriage of Sayyidah Fatimah and Sayyiduna Ali

With regard to the wedding (*Nikah*), the Prophet Muhammad ﷺ gathered his companions and gave each specific duties. For example, Umm al-Mu'minin Aisha helped Sayyidah Fatimah, and the Prophet ﷺ gave Sayyiduna Abu Bakr al-Siddique some money to go with Sayyiduna Salman al-Farisi and Sayyiduna Bilal to the marketplace to buy some necessities for the wedding. It is related that some of these items included a leather mat, a Khaybarian cloak, jars for food and water, a curtain, a veil, a bed, a mat, a copper container and a water skin. Sayyiduna Ali himself said, "All I had was the camel skin that I used to sleep on and cover myself with."

It was narrated that Sayyidah Aisha and Sayyidah Umm Salamah said, "The Messenger of Allah ﷺ commanded us (the wives of the Prophet) to prepare Fatimah (for her wedding) and take her in to Ali. We went to the house and sprinkled it with soft earth from the land of Batha. Then we stuffed two pillows with (datepalm) fibre which we picked with our own hands. Then we offered dates and raisins to eat, and sweet water to drink. We went and got some wood and set it up at the side of the room, to hang the clothes and water skins on, and we never saw any wedding better than the wedding of Fatimah."[215]

In an authentic hadith it is narrated that the Prophet ﷺ himself fitted out the home of his daughter prior to marriage. Ali said, "The Messenger of Allah ﷺ fitted out Fatimah with a velvet dress, a water-skin and a pillow stuffed with lemon grass and palm fibres."[216]

Allah ﷻ says, ***"And those, who, when they spend, are neither extravagant nor miserly, but hold to a middle path between those extremes,"*** (Q.25:67) and, ***"Let the rich man spend according to his means, and the man whose resources are restricted, let him spend according to what Allah has given him. Allah puts no burden on any person beyond what He has given him."*** (Q.65:7)

In a *sahih* hadith the Messenger of Allah ﷺ says, *"The best of dowries is the simplest,"*[217] and in another *sahih* hadith he ﷺ also says, *"The best of marriage is the simplest."*[218]

With regard to the dowry itself, Allah says, ***"And give women their dowries as a free gift but if they, of their own good pleasure, remit any part of it to you, take it, and enjoy it without fear of any harm (as Allah has made it lawful)."*** (Q.4:4)

The Messenger of Allah ﷺ also said, *"From among all the conditions which you have to fulfill, the conditions which make it legal for you to have sexual relations have the greatest right to be fulfilled."*[219]

Allah ﷻ is very strict in this regard when He says, ***"And even if you have given one of them a heap of gold, do not take any of it back,"*** (Q.4:20) but, ***"There is no blame on you about what you mutually agree after what is appointed of dowry."*** (Q.4:24)

To be even more clear, in the *Muwatta* of Imam Malik it reads, "Yahya related to me from Malik from Yahya ibn Said from Said ibn al-Musayyab that Umar ibn al-Khattab decided about the woman who was married by a man and the marriage had been consummated, that the bride-price was obligatory."[220]

In another narration Sahl ibn Sa'd narrated that the Prophet ﷺ said, *"Marry, even with (a Mahr equal to) an iron ring."*[221]

In an authentic hadith, it was narrated that Abdullah ibn Abbas said, "When Ali married Fatimah the Messenger of Allah ﷺ said to him, *'Give her something.'* He said, 'I do not have anything.' The Prophet said, *'Where is your armor that was made by the tribe of Hutama?'* "[222]

In the *Tabaqat* of ibn Sa'd it reads, "Ali married Fatimah and he sold a camel he had for about 480 *dirhams*[223] and Allah knows best. The exact amount is disputed, however what we do know is that with the sale of the armor and the camel, Sayyiduna Ali had enough of a dowry now for his beloved wife Fatimah al-Zahrah."

By doing this Ali ibn Abi Talib fulfilled his sacred right, as the Prophet ﷺ said, *"The best amongst you is the one who pays the rights of others generously."*[224]

Sayyiduna Ali, himself, speaks about his journey to get his *mahr* (dowry) for Fatimah. He said, "I got a she-camel as my share of the booty from the Battle of Badr and the Messenger of Allah ﷺ gave me another she-camel. I let both of them kneel at the door of one of the Ansar, having intended to pack lemon-grass on it to sell so that I could raise the money for my wedding banquet on marrying Fatimah. A goldsmith from Banu Qaynuqah was with me when we went to go see Hamzah ibn Abd al-Muttalib."[225]

The Wedding Feast

In the *Muwatta* of Imam Malik it reads that the Messenger of Allah ﷺ said, *"When you are invited to a wedding feast, you must go to it."*[226]

According to historians, the wedding of Sayyiduna Ali ibn Abi Talib and Fatimah al-Zahrah was not extravagant at all. The feast itself, being modest, was showing society that an extravagant wedding was not necessary to achieve love or success. It is only love that bonds the couple together, not worldly means, money or the promise of rank and status. The food at the banquet was very simple and consisted of healthy and beneficial foods, such as dates, milk and the like.

Abu Hurayrah said, "The worst food is the food of a wedding feast to which the rich are invited and the poor are left out. If anyone rejects an invitation, he has rebelled against Allah and His Messenger ﷺ."[227]

All the preparations for the marriage of Fatimah were done by Sayyidah Aisha (and the other wives of the Prophet ﷺ). Sayyidah Aisha said, "I have not seen a wedding better than that of the wedding of Fatimah."[228]

As was noted, right before the wedding, the Messenger of Allah ﷺ said, *"Allah, praised is His Name, Sublime is His Might, has made marriage the means towards maintaining a family line, and a matter whereby He enjoined to link the relations and He made it an obligation on His servants, saying,* ***'He it is Who created man from (congealed) water then He established relationships of lineage and marriage: for thy Lord has power (over all things).'*** " (Q.25:54)

The Prophet Muhammad ﷺ taught his daughter well throughout her life as is noted by Muadh ibn Jabal, who narrates that the Prophet ﷺ said, *"Don't cause your husband suffering,"* and, *"O my beloved Fatimah! reproach awaits the woman who disobeys her husband."*[229]

Likewise the Prophet ﷺ gave similar advice to everyone. The companions asked the Prophet ﷺ, "What do you say (command) about our wives?" He replied, *"Give them food what you have for yourself, and clothe them by which you clothe yourself, and do not beat them, and do not revile them."*[230]

In an important hadith, Abdullah ibn Umar narrated that the Prophet ﷺ said, *"The greatest sin amongst all sins in the eyes of Allah, is of a person, who marries a woman and divorces her once his needs have been fulfilled and also usurps her dowry in the process. Secondly, is a person who after having employed somebody usurps their pay. Thirdly, is a person who kills animals for no apparent reason."*[231]

During the wedding, the Prophet ﷺ said, *"Allah has commanded me to marry Fatimah the daughter of Khadijah to Ali ibn Abi Talib,"* then he ordered a platter of unripe dates to be brought to him of which we ate, and while we were eating Ali entered, whereupon the Prophet ﷺ smiled in his face and said, *"Allah has commanded me to marry you to Fatimah for (the dowry of) four hundred* (or five hundred according to other traditions) *ounces of silver if you agree."* Ali said, "I agree to that, O Messenger of Allah!" So, Ali sold his armor to get the money needed for his wedding. This is reported by Imam al-Tabari in his *Tarikh al-Tabari* from Anas who said, "By Allah, a great deal of good did indeed come out of them both." It is said that the light weight of the silver was to change the mentality of society in regard to the prevalent custom of high-priced dowries.

During the wedding the Prophet ﷺ recommended the husband to be kind to his bride and to comfort her by offering her something to drink when they meet the first time after the wedding.

He also said, *"On the night of the wedding, the husband should place his hand upon his wife's head and offer a supplication for her."*

One such supplication is, "O Allah! I ask of you the good of her and the good of what you have placed in her nature, and I seek refuge with you from the bad in her and the bad that you have placed in her nature."[232]

It is also said that one should perform two *rakat* and after performing the two cycles of prayer you supplicate:

"O Allah! Bless me with her affection, love and her acceptance of me; and make me pleased with her, and bring us together in the best form of a union and in absolute harmony; surely You like lawful things and dislike unlawful things."

The Prophet ﷺ recommended the couple to start every intercourse by saying: *In the Name of Allah, the Most-Gracious, the Most-Merciful* and by praying to Allah ﷻ to protect them (the couple) from the devil, and to protect the child from the devil if a child comes from that (particular) intercourse.[233]

One of the lessons which we should draw from the marriage of Ali and Fatimah is that they married one another because of their love of Islam. Allah ﷻ says, ***"My Lord! Grant me the power and ability that I may be grateful for Your Favour which You have bestowed upon me and upon my parents, and that I may do righteous good deeds, such as please You, and make my offspring good. Truly, I have turned to You in repentance, and truly, I am one of the Muslims (submitting to Your Will)."*** (Q.46:15)

Much more can be said, yet brevity is sunnah and with Allah ﷻ is the success.

Chapter 19:

The Home of Sayyidah Fatimah

In this chapter I will highlight some of the values that characterized the home of Sayyidah Fatimah before I recount stories that exemplify those values.

Asceticism [Zuhd]

In life we all at some point may worry about our finances, but it should never take us away from our goal of worshipping our Lord, for truly among the names of Allah ﷻ is *al-Razzaq*[234] and *al-Rahim*[235].

Many people may abort their children due to this fear and this is a big problem that has now spread throughout the world.

Allah ﷻ says, ***"And kill not your children from fear of poverty. We provide for them and for you. Surely, the killing of them is a great sin."*** (Q.17:31)

Abul Husayn al-Farisi said, "Do not worry about your sustenance, which is secured for you, but do the work you have taken upon yourself. This is the way of the *fata* and of the generous."[236]

Imam Sahl ibn Abdullah said, "Five things express the beauty of a being: when the poor appear rich; when the hungry appear satisfied; when those with heavy hearts appear joyful; when love is shown to an enemy; when feebleness does not appear despite fasting the whole day and praying the whole night."[237]

Abdullah ibn Abbas recounted, "Whoever had a female who was not buried nor insulted by him, and had not preferred his male children to her, Allah admits him to Paradise."[238]

Allah ﷻ says, ***"Let the rich man spend according to his means, and the man whose resources are restricted, let him spend according to what Allah has given him. Allah puts no burden on any person beyond what He has given him."*** (Q.65:7)

Imam Ahmad ibn Hanbal said, "The Prophet ﷺ would wake in the morning and his family would have nothing to eat and go to bed at night and they would have nothing to eat, [yet] he died married to nine wives, he chose marriage and encouraged others to marry."[239]

On the authority of Abu al-Abbas Sahl ibn Sa'd as-Saidi who said, "A man came to the Prophet ﷺ and said, 'O Messenger of Allah ﷺ, direct me to an act which, if I do it, it will cause Allah to love me and the people to love me.' He said, *'Renounce the world and Allah will love you, and renounce what people possess and people will love you.'* "[240]

Umar ibn al-Khattab narrated that the Prophet Muhammad ﷺ said, *"If you have proper and sincere reliance on Allah, He will provide you with provision, as He has provided the birds with provision, they come out of their nests in the morning with empty stomachs and return to their nests in the evening with a full stomach."*[241]

Even when times are bleak and we feel that none can help us, Allah ﷻ surely does say, ***"And whoever fears Allah, for him Allah brings forth a way out, and gives him provision [Rizq] from where he does not even imagine."*** (Q.65:2-3)

Imam al-Bukhari records in his *Sahih,* "A man passed by the Messenger of Allah ﷺ and he asked (his companions), *'What do you say about this rich man?'* They replied, 'If he asks for a lady's hand, he ought to be given her in marriage; and if he intercedes (for someone) his intercession should be accepted; and if he speaks, he should be listened to.' The Messenger of Allah ﷺ kept silent, and then a man from among the poor Muslims passed by, and he asked (them) *'What do you say about this man?'* They replied, 'If he asks for a lady's hand in marriage he does not deserve to be married, and if he intercedes (for someone), his intercession should not be accepted; and if he speaks, he should not be listened to.' The Messenger of Allah ﷺ said, *'This poor man is better than so many of the first as filling the earth.'* "[242]

Benefits of Marriage and Good Etiquette between Spouses

Allah ﷻ says, ***"And of everything We have created pairs, in order that you may remember."*** (Q.51:49)

Abdullah ibn Abbas said, "Allah has commanded (the Muslims) to get married, and He has encouraged and enticed them for it. So He has commanded to marry off their free-men and servants, and He has then promised them richness as a result."

"And Allah has made for you in your homes an abode." (Q.16:80) Hafidh ibn Kathir said, "In this verse of the Qur'an, Allah is mentioning His complete blessings upon His slaves in that he has given them homes which are a peaceful abode to them, to which they retreat and they seek refuge. They retreat to their homes as a haven and place of solace which covers them and gives them all kinds of benefits."

Part of this benefit is that, *"Whenever the son of Adam dies his actions stop except three: 1) knowledge that benefits people, 2) a recurring charity, and 3) a righteous child that supplicates for his parent."*[243]

Allah ﷻ says, ***"And live with them honorably. If you dislike them, it may be that you dislike a thing and Allah brings through it a great deal of good."*** (Q.4:19)

The Messenger of Allah ﷺ said, *"The believer should not harbor hatred towards his wife. If he dislikes something in her, then surely he will be pleased with another quality in her."*[244]

The Messenger of Allah ﷺ said, *"The most perfect of the believers in faith is the one who is best in attitude, and the best of you is the one who is best in attitude towards his womenfolk,"*[245] and in another version, *"The best among you are those who behave best toward their wives. I am the best among you toward his wives. The best among you is the one who is the kindest to his wife and the worst among you is the one who treats his wife badly."*[246]

On another occasion, Abdullah said, "We were with the Prophet ﷺ while we were young and had no wealth whatsoever. So the Messenger of Allah ﷺ said, *'O young people! Whoever among you can marry, should marry, because it helps him lower his gaze and guard his modesty, and whoever is not able to marry, should fast, as fasting diminishes his sexual power.' "*[247]

The Messenger of Allah ﷺ also stated, *"When someone with whose religion and character you are satisfied asks your daughter in marriage, accede to his request. If you do not do so, there will be temptation on Earth and extensive corruption."*[248]

One must note that poverty should not block a marriage between suitable partners. Sayyidah Fatimah and Sayyiduna Ali were poor in terms of material goods, however their spirit was rich in faith and contentment.

Allah ﷻ tells us that there is no need to worry, and remember when your Lord proclaimed, ***"If you are grateful, I will surely increase you in favor."*** (Q.14:7)

The Messenger of Allah ﷺ also gave us the roadmap of success when he said, *"Love Allah for what He nourishes you with of His blessings, and love me due to [this] love of Allah, and love my Ahlul Bayt due to [your having] love of me."*[249]

Worrying about provision is one of the downfalls in life and at times it can make people do something they normally would not. However, Allah ﷻ says that we should stay calm at such times, trusting in Him.

Allah ﷻ says, ***"Allah has favored some of you over others with regards to provision."*** (Q.16:1)

Among the provision Allah ﷻ provides is a good spouse; this is verified by the fact that the Prophet ﷺ said, *"A righteous wife to help you with your worldly and religious affairs is the best treasure anyone could have."*[250]

The husband must know that *"You never spend anything but you will be rewarded for it, even the morsel of food that you lift to your wife's mouth."*[251]

The Prophet ﷺ said, stating the basic rights of women, *"You are obliged to provide them with food and clothes honorably."*[252]

Therefore, we must conclude that there is a clear misconception on what the meaning of provision [*rizq*] is. Some may think that provision is solely money or how much material wealth you bring home for your family. However, this is clearly not the only definition of provision, for the Prophet ﷺ told the companion Abu Sa'id al-Khudri, *"Poverty for those of you who love me flows quicker than a flood from a mountain's peak to its base."*[253]

It was narrated that Abu Hurayrah said, "The Messenger of Allah ﷺ said, *'For one of you to chop wood and carry it on his back is better for him than asking (begging) from anyone who will either give him something or refuse to give him anything.'* "[254]

To show another example, a type of provision that is often overlooked by humanity is the fact that Allah ﷻ has given us life itself.

Allah ﷻ says, ***"We created man from a mingled drop to test him, and We made him hearing and seeing,"*** (Q.76:2) and, ***"Then formed the drop into a clot and formed the clot into a lump and formed the lump into bones and clothed the bones in flesh; and then brought him into being as another creature. Blessed be Allah, the Best of Creators!"*** (Q.23:14)

Allah ﷻ continues, ***"He creates you stage by stage in your mothers' wombs in threefold darkness. That is Allah, your Lord. Sovereignty is His. There is no god but Him. So what has made you deviate?"*** (Q.39:6)

"And We have enjoined on man (to be dutiful and good) to his parents. His mother bore[255] ***him in weakness and hardship upon weakness and hardship, and his weaning is in two years. Give thanks to Me and to your parents, unto Me is the final destination."*** (Q.31:14)

"It is He who created you, fashioned you perfectly, and made you balanced with the right proportions, in order for you to walk upright. In whatever form He willed, He put you together." (Q.82:7-8)

On top of this, Allah ﷻ promised to provide the necessary means for the family when He says, *"And eat of the things which Allah has provided for you, as lawful and good, and keep your duty to Allah in whom you believe."* (Q.5:88)

"Allah is the Provider, the one who has the Ultimate Power, the All-Mighty." (Q.53:58)

We are not singled out for this treatment, all of humanity and creation itself are under the protection and care of Allah ﷻ, *"There is no creature on the earth which is not dependent upon Allah for its provision."* (Q.11:6)

We will now go through the stories and examples of Sayyidah Fatimah al-Zahrah in order to extract the jewels and lessons therein. You will see that the verses and narrations above about *zuhd* and good etiquette between spouses, permeate the lives of Sayyidah Fatimah and Sayyiduna Ali.

The Verse of Feeding

Allah ﷻ says, ***"The righteous truly drink of a cup tempered with camphor – A fountain from which the servants of Allah drink, making it flow in abundance. They fulfil vows and fear a day, the evil of which is widespread. And they give food, out of love for Him, to the poor and the orphan and the captive. We feed you, for Allah's pleasure only – We desire from you neither reward nor thanks. Surely we fear from our Lord a stern, distressful day. So Allah will ward off from them the evil of that day, and cause them to meet with splendor and happiness; And reward them, for their steadfastness, with a Garden and with silk."*** (Q.76:5-12)

These verses of the Qur'an speak of Sayyiduna Fatimah al-Zahrah, Sayyiduna Ali ibn Abi Talib and their two sons Imams al-Hasan and al-Husayn.

Abdullah ibn Abbas narrates that once Imams al-Hasan and al-Husayn fell ill and the Prophet ﷺ, together with some of his companions, visited his sick grandsons. He suggested that Sayyiduna Ali should make a vow to Allah ﷻ for his sons' health. Heeding the Prophet's ﷺ suggestion, Ali, Fatimah and their maid Fidda, took a vow that if the boys recovered, they would fast for three consecutive days. Eventually they recovered and to fulfill the vow they also fasted along with their parents and maid. Since there was nothing in the house to eat, Sayyiduna Ali borrowed three measures of barley. Sayyidah Fatimah ground one measure into flour and baked it into five loaves (of bread) equal to their number, and placed these before them for breaking the fast. Just then a beggar stopped at their door and said, "Peace be upon you, O *Ahlul Bayt* of Muhammad! I am one of the poorest of Muslims, so can you please feed me and may Allah feed you of the food of Paradise!" So they gladly gave him all the food they had and slept that night, tasting nothing but water. They fasted again the next day and at sunset as they placed the bread before them to break the fast, an orphan knocked on the door asking for food and they cheerfully fed him, themselves going without food for yet another day. On the third day as the time to break their fast was approaching (and the food was spread out before them), a prisoner of war suddenly appeared at their door and the same scenario was repeated, with the Prophet's ﷺ *Ahlul Bayt* passing a third night without tasting a morsel of food. When dawn broke, Ali, holding the hands of al-Hasan and al-Husayn, came to the Prophet's ﷺ house. The Prophet, ﷺ seeing their pale countenances and noting that they were trembling from hunger, expressed dismay and at once accompanied them to their house. On entering the house, he was shocked to see the sight of his daughter Fatimah, sitting hollow-eyed on her prayer mat, her stomach sunk into her back. It was then that the angel Jibreel came down with this verse, saying, "O (Prophet) Muhammad, Allah congratulates you for (the sacrifice of) your household." Then he recited the abovementioned verse of feeding.

Turning Six Dirhams into Sixty Dirhams

On another occasion, Ubaydullah ibn Muhammad ibn Aisha narrates that when a beggar came to Sayyiduna Ali, he said to (his son) Imam al-Hasan or al-Husayn, "Go to your mother and tell her to give one of the six *dirhams* that I had left with her."

His son went and later returned with the message that she said, "You had left the six *dirhams* to purchase flour." Sayyiduna Ali said, "The iman of a person cannot be true until he has more trust in that which is in Allah's hands than that which is in his hands." He then sent a message to her to send all six *dirhams*. When she did so, he gave it all to the beggar.

Sayyiduna Ali had not yet even changed his posture when a man arrived selling a camel. "How much for the camel?" Sayyiduna Ali asked. "A hundred and forty *dirhams,*" the man replied. Sayyiduna Ali told the man to tie the camel for him with the understanding that he would pay for it after a while. The man tied the camel there and then left. Another man then passed by and asked who the camel belonged to. When Sayyiduna Ali informed him that the camel was his, the man asked him whether he would sell it. "Certainly," replied Sayyiduna Ali. "How much?", he asked. "For two hundred *dirhams,*" was the reply. The man agreed to buy it, handed over the two hundred *dirhams* and then took the camel.

Sayyiduna Ali then paid a hundred and forty *dirhams* to the man whom he had promised to pay and then returned with sixty *dirhams* to (his wife) Sayyidah Fatimah. Seeing the money she asked, "What is this?" Ali replied, "This is what Allah promised us on the lips of His Prophet ﷺ, ***'Whoever brings (carries out) a good act will receive ten times as much.'***" (Q.6:160)

"Allah gives sustenance to whom He wills, without reckoning." (Q.3:37)

Tasbeeh Fatimah

Part of the struggle of Sayyidah Fatimah al-Zahrah is that when Sayyiduna Ali was travelling, busy at work, or accompanying the Messenger of Allah ﷺ, she would have to take care of the home by herself. She would clean, cook and care for the children, among other responsibilities. Because of these hardships, she asked her father for a maid in order to ease some of the burden of the household.

There is a narration in this regard and it reads, "Sayyiduna Ali ibn Abi Talib said, 'Fatimah went to the Prophet ﷺ complaining of her hands blistering, so he ordered her to say the Tasbeeh, Takbir, and Tahmid (Tasbeeh Fatimah).' "[256]

The reason the Prophet ﷺ gave his daughter something spiritual was to teach the family that this life was not about ease and comfort, it is about struggle and putting others first. For patiently bearing the struggle, Allah ﷻ united Sayyidah Fatimah and Lady Fidda and they helped each other around the house.

In another version Sayyiduna Ali ibn Abi Talib narrates himself that "Sayyidah Fatimah came to the Prophet ﷺ asking for a maid. The Prophet ﷺ said, *'May I inform you of something better than that? When you go to bed, recite Subhan Allah 33 times, Alhamdulillah 33 times, and Allahu Akbar 34 times.'*" Sayyiduna Ali added, "I have never failed to recite it since." Somebody asked, "Even on the night of the Battle of Siffin?" He said, "Yes, even on the night of the Battle of Siffin."[257]

This is the same Tasbeeh Fatimah that we all are encouraged to do after every obligatory prayer and before going to sleep. May Allah ﷻ increase us by means of it and with Allah ﷻ is the success.

The Lesson of the Curtain

On another occasion, Abdullah ibn Umar narrates that when the Messenger of Allah ﷺ set out on a journey, the last person he would speak to from his family before setting off would be Fatimah. When he returned from a journey, the first person the Prophet ﷺ would come to would be Fatimah.[258] After returning from one of his journeys, the Prophet ﷺ came to Sayyidah Fatimah and found a beautiful curtain hanging at her door, so he did not enter. Then Ali came and found that Sayyidah Fatimah was upset. He asked, "What is the matter with you?" She replied, "The Messenger of Allah ﷺ came to me but did not enter the house." Ali then came to him and said, "Messenger of Allah ﷺ, Fatimah took it the wrong way that you came to visit her but did not go in." He replied, *"What have I to do with this world? What have I to do with extremely decorated curtains and the like?"* He (Ali) then went to Fatimah and informed her of what the Messenger of Allah ﷺ had said. She said, "Ask the Messenger of Allah ﷺ what he wants me to do about it." He ﷺ said, *"Tell her that she must send it to so-and-so."*[259]

A Lesson in Reliance upon Allah

Sayyiduna Ali woke up one morning and asked Sayyidah Fatimah, "Do you have anything to give me for lunch?" She replied, "No, by Him who honoured my father with prophethood, I have nothing to give you, and for these last two days we have had nothing except I gave to you and these two boys of mine instead of myself." Sayyiduna Ali said, "Why did you not tell me so that I might find something for you?" She replied, "I was too shy before Allah to burden you with something you could not bear."

So he left her and went out, trusting in Allah ﷻ and thinking the best of Him, and borrowed a *dinar*. As he was looking to buy something for his family, he saw al-Miqdad. It happened to be a very hot day and the sun had burned him from above and hurt him from below. When Sayyiduna Ali saw him, he said, "O Miqdad, what made you go out at this time?" He replied, "Abul-Hasan, let me go my way, and ask me not what is behind me." "Son of my brother," he said, "It is not permissible to conceal your situation from me." So al-Miqdad said, "If you insist, then by Him who honoured Muhammad with prophethood, I only came out because I had to. I left my family crying with hunger, for when I heard my dependents crying I could not bear to stay. Thus, I went out in a state of distress, wandering blindly. This is my situation and my story." Sayyiduna Ali started to weep until the tears wet his beard. "I swear by the One by whom you swore that I have come out for the very same reason. I borrowed a *dinar*, so here, take it. I'd rather you had it than me." Sayyiduna Ali gave al-Miqdad the *dinar* and turned back, heading for the mosque of the Prophet ﷺ and remaining there for the midday, afternoon and sunset prayers.

When the Prophet ﷺ had finished the sunset prayer, he passed by Sayyiduna Ali in the front row and touched him with his foot. Sayyiduna Ali sprang up, followed the Prophet ﷺ to the door of the mosque and greeted him. The Prophet ﷺ returned his greeting and said, *"O Abul-Hasan, do you have anything to give us for dinner so that I might go with you?"* Sayyiduna Ali remained silent, not knowing how to answer, because of his shyness before the Prophet ﷺ, who knew the situation that had led him to come out. When the Prophet ﷺ saw Sayyiduna Ali's silence he said, *"O Abul-Hasan, what is the matter? Will you not tell me no, so that I may leave you, or tell me yes, so that I may come with you?"* Then out of pure love and kindness, he said, *"Nay, let us be off!"* For Allah ﷻ revealed to His Prophet ﷺ that he would eat with them that night.

Sayyiduna Ali agreed, and the Prophet ﷺ took his hand and they went off together to the house, finding Sayyidah Fatimah in her prayer room after having prayed, with a pot behind her giving off steam. When she heard the Prophet's ﷺ voice in the house, she came out of the prayer room and greeted him. She was the dearest of all people to him, and he returned her greeting, rubbed her head with his hand and said, *"How are you this evening? May Allah have mercy on you! Give us our dinner and may Allah forgive you – which He surely has!"* She took the pot and put it in front of him. When Sayyiduna Ali saw the pot and smelled its fragrance, he gave Sayyidah Fatimah a harsh look. "How harsh is your look, and how cruel!" she said. "Glory be to Allah! Have I committed any sin against you that would merit such anger?" Sayyiduna Ali replied, "Did you not swear by Allah, the last time I saw you, that you had not eaten for two days?" She looked to the heavens and said, "My God knows, in His heaven and on His earth, that I spoke naught but the truth!" So Sayyiduna Ali asked, "Then whence came you this, the like of which I have never seen nor smelt, nor have I ever eaten anything finer?"

The Prophet ﷺ placed his blessed hand between Sayyiduna Ali's shoulders, moved it from side to side, and said, *"O Ali, this is the reward for your dinar. This is recompense for your dinar. This is from Allah:* ***Allah gives His sustenance to whom He will, without reckoning.****"* (Q.3:37) The Prophet ﷺ then wept, saying, *"Praise be to Allah, who refused to let the two of you leave this world without first making you [Ali] experience what He made Maryam experience:* ***Whenever Zakariyya came to her in the sanctuary, he found she had sustenance.****"* (Q.3:37)[260]

Sacrifing That Which You Love

Before the marriage of Sayyidah Fatimah, the Prophet ﷺ bought her a new dress for her marriage ceremony. The day before her wedding a person knocked on her door seeking help. Sayyidah Fatimah did not have anything to give this poor and needy person so decided to give away her wedding dress.

The following day, at her wedding, she wore an old dress. Seeing this the Prophet ﷺ inquired about her wedding dress. She explained that she had decided to give it away in obedience to the verse, ***"Never will you attain righteousness until you spend in the way of Allah from that which you love. And whatever you spend – indeed, Allah is Knowing of it."*** (Q.3:92)

The Blessed Necklace

Jabir bin Abdullah al-Ansari related, "One day, we were with the Prophet ﷺ after Asr prayer when an old immigrant man came by, wearing worn out clothes and due to old age and weakness was barely able to walk. The Prophet ﷺ inquired about his welfare and the old man said, 'O Prophet of Allah! I am starving, so feed me; I am naked, so clothe me; and I am poor, so help me!'

"The Prophet ﷺ said, *'I have nothing to give you, yet he who guides to goodness is equal to one who performs it. So go to the house of one who loves Allah and His Messenger, and Allah and His Messenger love her. The one who prefers Allah over herself; I mean Fatimah'.*

"The Prophet ﷺ asked Bilal to lead the old man to her house. As soon as they reached her house, the old man cried out, 'Peace be upon you O People of the House! Where the angels frequent their visits; where Jibril descends bringing what the Lord of the Worlds reveals.'

"Sayyidah Fatimah responded to his greetings and asked who he was, to which the old man replied, 'I am an old Arab man. I have emigrated to your father from a distant land. O daughter of Muhammad! I am hungry and in need of clothing, so console me and may Allah bless you!'

"This incident occurred at a time when the Messenger of Allah ﷺ, Sayyiduna Ali and Sayyidah Fatimah had not eaten anything for three days. Fatimah gave the old man a ram skin which was used as a bed by her two children, al-Hasan and al-Husayn.

"However, the old man said, 'O daughter of Muhammad! I complain to you of hunger and you give me a ram's skin? How can I eat this?' Fatimah took out her necklace which Fatimah bint Hamzah bin Abd al-Muttalib had given to her, handed it over to the old man saying, 'Sell this and Allah will provide you with a solution to your problem.'

"The old man took the necklace and showed it to the Messenger of Allah ﷺ, who said, *'Indeed Allah will grant you a solution, for Fatimah, the Liege lady of all the women has given to you this necklace.'* Ammar bin Yassir, who was present, said, 'O Messenger of Allah ﷺ! Do you allow me to buy this necklace?' The Prophet ﷺ said, *'Buy it Ammar, surely if all men and women participate in its purchase, Allah will protect them from Hellfire.'*

"Ammar asked the old man for its price and he replied, 'A meal of bread and meat, a Yemeni shirt to cover myself and a *dinar* to return to my family.' Ammar gave him 20 *dinars* and 200 *dirhams*, a Yemeni shirt, wheat bread and meat, and a horse to take him to his home.

"The Prophet ﷺ asked the old man if he was satisfied with all that and he replied in affirmation. *'So reward Fatimah for her kindness!'* said the Messenger of Allah ﷺ. The old man prayed, 'O Allah! Give Fatimah that which no eye has seen and no ear has heard.'

"Ammar perfumed the necklace with musk and sent it to the Prophet ﷺ with a slave whom he had purchased with the booty he received from Khaybar, saying, 'Give this necklace to the Messenger of Allah ﷺ and tell him that I gift you to him too.' When the slave delivered the necklace and the message, the Prophet ﷺ said to him, *'Take this necklace to Fatimah and I gift you to her'.*

"When the slave came to Sayyidah Fatimah, she took her necklace back and set the slave free. When the slave was set free, he laughed loudly. Sayyidah Fatimah asked him the reason for his laughing and he said, 'I laughed when I thought of the abundance of goodness in this necklace. It fed a hungry man, it clothed a naked man, satisfied a poor man, freed a slave, and came back to its original owner.' "

Much more can be said, yet brevity is sunnah and with Allah ﷺ is the success.

Chapter 20:

The Passing of Sayyidah Fatimah

In the year 10AH the Prophet ﷺ passed away. During his last illness Sayyidah Fatimah would constantly attend to the Prophet ﷺ.

Sayyidah Aisha narrates, "I have not seen anyone closer in conduct, way, and manners to that of the Messenger of Allah ﷺ in regards to standing and sitting, than Fatimah the daughter of the Messenger of Allah ﷺ. Whenever she would enter upon the Prophet ﷺ he would stand for her and kiss her, and he would sit her in his sitting place. Whenever the Prophet ﷺ entered upon her she would stand from her seat, and kiss him and sit him in her sitting place. So when the Prophet ﷺ fell sick and Fatimah entered, she bent over and kissed him. Then she lifted her head and cried, then she bent over him and she lifted her head and laughed. So I said, 'I used to think that this one was from the most intelligent of our women, but she is really just one of the women.' So when the Prophet ﷺ died, I said to her, 'Do you remember when you bent over the Prophet ﷺ and you lifted your head and cried, then you bent over him, then you lifted your head and laughed. What caused you to do that?' She said, 'He ﷺ told me that he was to die from his illness, so I cried. Then he told me that I would be the quickest of his family to meet up with him. So that is when I laughed.' "

Such was her sorrow at the passing of her beloved father, the following line of poetry is attributed to her:

> The horizons have dimmed, the sun diminished;
> The light of the afternoon has darkened.
> After the Prophet, the earth has gone into mourning,
> Quaking and crying out in its grief.
> Weep, O eastern and western lands!
> Weep, O Mudar and Yaman!
> Weep, O mighty mountain!
> Weep, O House of curtains and pillars!
> O Seal of Messengers, bearer of holy light,
> May He who sent down the Qur'an Bless you![261]

Around six months afterwards, Sayyidah Fatimah passed away. As she had already been told that she would be joining her father soon, she prepared for the moment.

It is narrated by ibn Sa'd that Salma said, "Fatimah, the daughter of the Messenger of Allah ﷺ, was ill while we were with her. On the day she died, Ali had gone out. She said to me, 'Pour a bath for me.' So I poured a bath for her and she washed in the best manner in which she used to wash. Then she said, 'Bring me my new clothes.' So I brought them to her and she put them on. Then she said, 'Put my bed in the middle of the house.' I did that and she lay down on it and faced the qibla. Then she said to me, 'Mother, I will die now. I have washed, so do not let anyone uncover my shoulder.' After this she died. Then Ali came and I told him. He said, 'By Allah, no one will uncover her shoulder.' He took and buried her with that ghusl."[262]

Her passing was on the 3rd of Ramadan in the year 11 Hijri. Imam al-Dhahabi said she was 24. Others have said she was 21, 26, 27, or 29 years old, and some have even put her age in the early 30s, and Allah ﷻ knows best.

Here ends the journey into the Mines of the *Ahlul-Kisa*. We hope that you have enjoyed this journey and have gathered many memorable jewels within. We hope to see you all on the next journey – *The Virtues of the Hasnayn, the Lives and Struggles of Imams al-Hasan and al-Husayn.*

This is why their lives have not been spoken of in the present volume and we ask Allah ﷻ for the time and strength to complete the journey.

Peace and Blessings of Allah be upon the Messenger of Allah ﷺ, his family and companions. The last of the call is Alhamdulillah, all praise is due to Allah.

"Then, to Allah belongs all praise – Lord of the heavens and Lord of the earth, Lord of the worlds." (Q.45:36)[263]

Much more can be said, yet brevity is sunnah and with Allah ﷻ is the success.

Appendix 1:

Poem in Praise of Sayyidah Fatimah

O Umm al-Hassanain, by Walid Lounès Bouzerar

What blend of even the finest words
Can symbolise your worth?
O Umm al-Hassanain, through your Progeny,
Mercy from Heaven rains
The day this world was graced and raised
By your luminous, blessed birth
Was akin to a rare, lustrous flower
Plucked from Celestial plains

Every honored woman en route to Janna
Is guided by your fragrance
The musk of your purity intoxicates
Till all their troubles wane
The dwellers of Janna are enraptured
By your all-pervading radiance
Through love for your Family every blessing
In Dunya and Akhira is gained

Muhammad ﷺ, the Matchless Sapphire,
You are of him and he is of you
The daughter of the Foremost of Creation ﷺ,
Before you I am humbled in speech
Should the gold and gems of this world be gathered
They would not equal your due
Nor the due of a speck of dust that grazed
The soles of your blessed feet

O Allah – upon Your Prophet ﷺ
And his Precious Treasure, al-Zahra
Send Your Perfect Peace and Blessings
By the strength of their lofty Stations
Guide our mothers, sisters and daughters
By the hand of their Queen, Fatima
Make our love for her Family the sacred Crown
Of our Single Aspiration

Appendix 2:

Some Verses and Hadith About the Duty of Loving the Ahlul Bayt

1. ***"O people of the Prophetic household! Allah intends but to remove all sorts of uncleanness and blemish from you and to purify you with a thorough purification."*** (Q.33:33)

2. ***"Say: 'I do not ask you for any wage for this (meaning: conveying the Message and instructing others with the Guidance) except for you to love the near of kin.' "*** (Q.42:23)

Ibn Abbas said this means "except that you show love

to my kinsfolk and bear me in mind when dealing with them" i.e. through maintaining a connection with them, making them happy and showing respect and reverence to them.

Al-Hakim in *al-Mustadrak,* relates from Ibn Abbas when this verse was revealed, they (the companions) asked, "Messenger of Allah, who are your kinsfolk whom we have been ordered to love?" The Prophet ﷺ replied, *"Ali, Fatimah and their two sons"* and in another wording *"their children"*.

3. The Messenger of Allah ﷺ said, *"Indeed, I am leaving among you that which if you hold fast to them, you shall not be misguided after me. One of them is greater than the other, The Book of Allah is a rope extended from the sky to the earth, and my family – the people of my house – and they shall not split until they meet at the Hawd, so look at how you deal with them after me."*[264]

4. The Messenger of Allah ﷺ said, *"Love Allah for what He nourishes you with of His blessings, and love me due to this love of Allah, and love my Ahlul Bayt due to your having love of me."*[265]

5. The Messenger of Allah ﷺ said, *"The stars are a security for the residents of the heavens and my household are a security for the residents of earth."*[266]

6. The Messenger of Allah ﷺ said, *"Train your children to have three characteristics; love of your Prophet ﷺ, love of his family and recitation of the Qur'an."*[267]

7. The Messenger of Allah ﷺ said, *"To hate Banu Hashim and the Ansar is unbelief, and to hate the Arabs is hypocrisy."*[268]

8. The Messenger of Allah ﷺ said, *"Whoever obeys Ali, obeys me, whoever obeys me, obeys Allah, whoever disobeys Ali disobeys me, whoever disobeys me, disobeys Allah."*[269]

9. The Prophet ﷺ said to Ali, *"No one loves you except a believer, and no one hates you except a hypocrite."*[270]

10. The Prophet ﷺ said, *"By Him in Whose hand is my soul, no one hates us, the Ahlul Bayt, except that Allah will throw him down on his face in the Fire of Hell."*[271]

Appendix 3:

Names of Sayyidah Fatimah

Below is a list of names of Sayyidah Fatimah identified by Khwaja Shaykh Abdur Rahman Chohravi, in *Majmu'ah Salawat ur Rasul (A Compendium of Blessings on Prophet Muhammad* ﷺ*)*:

Sayyidah kulli nisa il-Janna – The leader of all the women in Paradise
Fatimah – The one removed from hellfire
al-Zahrah – The Resplendent
Batul – The Chaste
Sayyidah – The Leader
Masturah – The veiled / Chaste
Ma'sumah – Sinless
Marhumah – Enveloped in Allah's mercy
Raki'ah – The one who bows in worship to Allah
Sajidah – The one who prostrates in worship to Allah
Saimah – The one who fasts
Saniyah – The one safeguarded
Damiyah – Beautiful
Mukhaddarah – One who chooses seclusion
Zahidah – Ascetic
Abidah – One who worships Allah
Waliyyah – Saint
Wafiyya – Faithful
Baqiyyah – The only remaining child of the Prophet
Adfiyya – Warm-hearted
Taqiyya – Devout / God-fearing
Zakiyya – Pure
Radiyyah – Well pleased with Allah as her Lord

Mardiyyah – The one pleasing to Allah as His worshipper
Hulliyyah – Adorned, Beautified
Aliyyah – Elevated
Safiyyah – The Chosen
Salimah – Safe, Sound
Halima – Gentle, Forbearing
Raqiyyah – One who has ascended the heights
Hakima – The Wise
Hasibah – Of noble birth
Nasibah – Of noble lineage
Jamilah – Beautiful
Jalilah – Sublime / Majestic
Habibah – Beloved by all
Hasaniyyah – Naturally good
Mushfiqah – Compassionate
Sa'liha – Righteous
Salihah – Naturally pious
Sabihah – Pretty, Graceful
Musabbihah – One who glorifies Allah
Majdidah – One who praises Allah
Muhammadah – One who is praised
Muhassilah – The one who obtains the best results
Mukabbirah – One who proclaims Allah's Greatness
Qariyah – Reciter of the Qur'an
Mumajjidah – One who glorifies Allah
Jariya – Servant of Allah
Fadilah – Personification of virtue
Wasilah – A means to approach Allah
Nasibah – So fortunate
Najibah – Noble, Distinguished
Sharifah – Noble
Karimah – Generous
Mukarramah – Honoured
Alimah – Learned
Fatiha – The Opener (of doors of goodness)
Muhtaramah – Revered
Mu'ammah – Universally popular
Mu'allamah – Taught by the Prophet
Da'iyah – The one who invites to Islam
Shafi'ah – The one who intercedes to Allah
Shafi'ah – The one whose intercession is accepted by Allah
Ummiyyah – Exemplary Mother

Tahiyyah – The one who greets with good cheer
Nasihah – The one who gives good counsel
Rajihah – Most Favourable
Wahiyya – The one who receives Divine inspiration
Shahiyyah – Pleasant
Jahida – The one who exerts in the way of Allah
Mujtahidah – The one who strives in the way of Allah
Raqiyah – Of a high rank
Nasiyah – The cornerstone of the Muslim ummah
Awsiyah – The Best Advisor
Khawirah – Affectionate, Kindly
Khadira – The one who makes things evergreen
Waqiyah – The one who protects
Dafiyah – The one who mingles with the poor and oppressed
Sahibah – The Companion of the Prophet
Hawirah – Highly intelligent, promotes dialogue
Wajidah – The Finder, the one who found her father persecuted and helped him
Aqibah – Successor, the one who continues the good works of her father
Samiyah – Truthfully brave
Nur – Light
Bint Nur – The daughter of the one who is light
Bid'atu Rasul Sayyidina Muhammad – Part of the Messenger of Allah ﷺ

Endnotes

[1] It must be noted that the Prophet's cloak is a source of blessings. It is said that Aisha al-Siddiqah kept the cloak of the Prophet with her and Asma said she kept it with her after the death of Aisha in order for people to seek blessings by it. In *Sharh Sahih Muslim,* Imam al-Nawawi said, "This hadith is a proof that it is recommended to seek blessings through the relics and clothing of the righteous." Quote from Imam al-Nawawi as extracted from: Khalid Williams, *The Perfect Family – Virtues of the Ahl al-Bayt* (Visions of Reality, 2015), p.20.

[2] Imam al-Tirmidhi, *Sunan*. The hadith is narrated on the authority of Umar ibn Abi Salamah. Imam al-Dhahabi and Imam al-Hakim both state that this hadith is authentic.

[3] Imam Ahmad ibn Hanbal, *Musnad*. The hadith is narrated on the authority of Umm Salamah. In *Tafsir al-Durr al-Manthur* Imam Jalal al-Din al-Suyuti states, "The phrase, *'You are on the good path'*, or annexed with the expression 'You are one of the Prophet's wives' ". In *Tafsir ibn Kathir* it states, *"Stay where you are, you are on the good path."* In *al-Mustadrak ala-Sahihayn* Imam al-Hakim records, *"You are on the good path, and these are my Ahlul Bayt."* There is another hadith and it reads: Umm Salamah said, "It was in my house that these verses were revealed, ***'Allah intends but to remove all sorts of uncleanness and blemish from you and to purify you with a thorough purification.'*** So the Prophet called for Ali and Fatimah and al-Hasan and al-Husayn and then said, *'These are Ahlu-Bayti.'* [In the hadith of al-Qadi and al-Summi it reads, *'They are my family.'* (*Ahli*)] So I said, 'O Messenger of Allah! aren't I also from your Ahlul-Bayt?' He said, *'Yes you are Insha Allah.'* " This is from Imam al-Hakim and from Imam al-Bayhaqi in his *Sunan al-Kubra*. The rank of the hadith: the chain is authentic and all of its narrators are trustworthy.

[4] Imam Muslim, *Sahih*. This hadith is narrated on the authority of Aisha al-Siddiqah. In this specific case, meaning the Verse of Purification and the hadith *Ahlul-Kisa*, these of course are concerning Sayyidah Fatimah, Ali, al-Hasan and al-Husayn; however this does not mean that the wives of the Prophet Muhammad are not from the *Ahlul-Bayt*. One such hadith is from Anas ibn Malik, "I also saw the wedding feast of Zaynab, and he served bread and meat to the people, and made them eat to their heart's content, and he sent me to call people, and as he was free (from the ceremony) he stood up and I followed him. Two persons were left and they were busy in talking and did not get out (of the apartment). He then proceeded towards (the apartments of) his wives. He greeted with Assalaamu Alaykum to every one of them and said, *'Members of the household, how are you?'* They said, 'Messenger of Allah, we are in good state. How do you find your family?' He would say, *'In a good state.'* " This is transmitted by Imam Muslim in his *Sahih*. A similar narration is present in *Sahih al-Bukhari*; and in regard to those who think that this verse only applies to the *Ahlul-Kisa* then they use narrations such as this and others: "When the Messenger of Allah noticed that a blessing from Allah was to descend, he told Safiyya [one of his wives], *'Call for me! Call for me!'* Safiyyah asked, 'Call who, O Messenger of Allah?' He said, *'Call for me my Ahlul-Bayt who are Ali, Fatimah, al-Hasan, and al-Husayn.'* Thus we sent for them and they came to him. Then the Prophet spread his cloak (upper garment) over them, and raised his hand (toward sky) saying, *'O Allah! These are my family, so bless Muhammad and the family of Muhammad,'* " Imam al-Hakim, *Mustadrak*.

[5] *Diwan Imam ash-Shafi'i*. Translation extracted from Muhammad Jaffar al-Kattani, *al-Arba'in: On the Duty of Loving the Noble Family of the Prophet Muhammad,* trans. Safaruk Zaman Chowdhury, (London: Turath Publishing, 2010), p.68.

[6] Imam Abu Nu'aym, *Hilyat al-Awliyah.*

[7] Imam al-Tirmidhi, *Sunan.* This hadith is narrated on the authority of Abdullah ibn Abbas.

[8] Imam al-Tabarani, *Mu'jam al-Awsat.*

[9] Imam al-Tirmidhi, *Sunan.* This hadith is narrated on the authority of Abu Sa'id al-Khudri. Allah speaks of this within the Qur'an, ***"Surely those who believed and immigrated and struggled hard in the path of Allah with their property and their souls, and those who gave shelter and helped [Ansar] – these are guardians, friends [Awliyah] of each other."*** (Q.8:72)

[10] Imam ibn Asakir, *Tarikh al-Dimashq.*

[11] Imam ibn Athir, *al-Kamil fi al-Tarikh.*

[12] Imam Jalal al-Din al-Suyuti, *Imam al-Isfahani fi al-Targeeb kama fi Manahil al-Safa al-Suyuti.* This hadith is narrated on the authority of Anas ibn Malik.

[13] Imam ibn Sa'd, *Tabaqat ibn Sa'd.* Also related by Imam al-Tabari in *Sharaf al-Nubuwwa,* who narrates it on the authority of Abu Sa'id al-Khudri and Shaykh ibn Hajar al-Haytami in *al-Sawa'iq al-Muhriqah,* p.231.

[14] Shaykh ibn Hajar al-Haytami, *al-Sawa'iq al-Muhriqah,* pp.261-262; also related by Imam al-Bayhaqi and others.

[15] Imam ibn Abi Shaybah, *al-Musannaf.* This is a saying of Sayyiduna Ali ibn Abi Talib.

[16] Imam ibn Abi Shaybah, *al-Musannaf;* also found within *al-Durr al-Manthur fi Tafsir bil-Ma'thur* by Imam Jalal al-Din al-Suyuti. Some scholars, especially from the science of *Ilm al-Rijal,* do find fault with some of the chains, however this tradition is narrated by eight companions of the Prophet, and eight persons from the students of the companions, and by sixty scholars and more than ninety authors have quoted it in their books.

[17] Imam al-Hakim, *Mustadrak.*

[18] The Hadith of the Ark has been related by: Imam Muslim, *Sahih;* Imam Ahmad ibn Hanbal, *Musnad;* Imam Abu Nu'aym, *Hilyat al-Awliyah;* Imam Fakhr al-Din al-Razi, *Tafsir-e-Mafatihu'l-Ghaib;* Imam Jalal al-Din al-Suyuti, *Durr al-Manthur;* Imam al-Tabarani, *Mu'jam al-Awsat;* Imam al-Hakim, *Mustadrak* and Imam al-Tabari in his *Tafsir* as well as his *Tarikh al-Tabari.*

[19] Shaykh ibn Hajar al-Haytami said, "This is an authentic hadith and many scholars relate the variant narrations of hadith including Imam Muslim in his *Sahih.*" He also said, "The multiple chains strengthen one another."

[20] She is Sayyidah Fatimah bint Muhammad ibn Abdullah ibn Abd al-Muttalib (who was called Shaybatul Hamd) ibn Hashim (named Amr) ibn Abd Munaf (named al-Mughirah) ibn Qusayy (also called Zayd) ibn Kilaab ibn Murrah ibn Ka'b ibn Lu'ayy ibn Ghalib ibn Fahr (who was called Quraysh and whose tribe was named after him) ibn Malik ibn an-Nadr (also called Qays) ibn Kinanah ibn Khuzaymah ibn Mudrikah (who was called Amir) ibn Elias ibn Mudar ibn Nizar ibn Ma'ad ibn Adnan.

[21] Imam Jalal al-Din al-Suyuti, *al-Jami al-Saghir;* Shaykh ibn Hajar al-Haytami, *al-Sawaiq al-Muhariqah;* Shaykh Muttaqi al-Hindi, *Kanz al-Umal,* and by others.

[22] Imam al-Bukhari, *Sahih;* Imam Abu Nu'aym, *Hilyat al-Awliyah;* Shaykh Muttaqi al-Hindi, *Kanz al-Umal,* and Mirza Hindi, *Muntakhab Kanz al-Umal.*

[23] Imam Abu Nu'aym, *Hilyat al-Awliyah.*

[24] Imam al-Tirmidhi, *Sunan;* Imam al-Nasa'i, *al-Sunan al-Kubra;* Imam Ahmad ibn Hanbal, *Musnad;* Imam ibn Abi Shaybah, *al-Musannaf;* Imam al-Hakim, *Mustadrak,* and Imam al-Tabarani, *al-Mu'jam al-Kabir.*

[25] Hafidh al-Muwaffaq ibn Ahmad al-Makki al-Hanafi al-Khwarazim, *Maqtal al-Husayn*, p.67.

[26] The best swords of the time were Indian and the connection between the sword and light is that the Arabs signalled the way by standing on a rise and brandishing their swords in the sun so that they flashed like mirrors.

[27] Translation extracted from: Suzanne Pinckney Stetkevych, *The Mantle Odes: Arabic Praise Poems to the Prophet Muhammad* (Bloomington: Indiana University Press, 2010), p.48.

[28] Shaykh Abd al-Ghani al-Nablusi, *Hadiqa al-Nadiyyah*. This quote is extracted from: Shaykh Gibril Haddad, *The First Thing That Allah Created Was My Nur* www.livingislam.org/fiqhi/fiqha_e30.html. Accessed 26 October 2017.

[29] Other verses that mention this light are: ***"Have you not seen how Allah created seven heavens, one upon another, and set the moon therein for a light and the sun for a lamp?"*** (Q.71:16) and, ***"Blessed is He who has set in the sky constellations and has set among them a lamp and an illuminating moon."*** (Q.25:61)

[30] Imam al-Tirmidhi, *Sunan*.

[31] Sayyid Abu al-Hasan Ahmad ibn Abd Allah Bakri, *al-Anwar Fi Mawlid al-Nabi Muhammad Alayhi al-Salat wa al-Salam*. This quote is extracted from: Shaykh Gibril Haddad, *The First Thing That Allah Created Was My Nur* www.livingislam.org/fiqhi/fiqha_e30.html. Accessed 26 October 2017.

[32] Mullah Ali Qari, *The Quenching Source on the Birth of the Prophet* [*al-Mawrid al-Rawi Fi Mawlid al-Nabi*], trans. Abdul Aziz Suraqah (Ibriz Media, 2016), p.29.

[33] Shaykh Abd al-Qadir al-Jilani, *Secret of Secrets* [*Sirr al-Asrar Fi Ma Yahtaju Ilayhi al-Abrar*], trans. Shaykh Tosun Bayrak al-Jerrahi (Cambridge: The Islamic Texts Society, 1992), pp12-14.

[34] When Allah created Adam, He wiped Adam's back and every person that He will create from him until the Day of Resurrection fell out from his back. Allah placed a glimmering light between the eyes of each one of them. Allah showed them to Adam and Adam asked, "O Lord! Who are they?" Allah said, "These are your offspring." Adam saw a man from among them whose light he liked. He asked, "O Lord! Who is this man?" Allah said, "This is a man from the latter generations of your offspring. His name is Dawud." Adam said, "O Lord! How many years would he live?" Allah said, "Sixty years." Adam said, "O Lord! I have forfeited forty years from my life for him." When Adam's life came to an end, the angel of death came to him (to take his soul). Adam said, "I still have forty years from my life term, don't I?" He replied, "Have you not given it to your son Dawud?" So Adam denied this and his offspring followed suit (denying Allah's covenant), Adam forgot and his offspring forgot, Adam made a mistake and his offspring made mistakes. Imam al-Tirmidhi said, "This prophetic saying is authentic, and it was reported from various chains of narration through Abu Hurayrah from the Prophet." Imam al-Hakim also recorded it in his *Mustadrak*, and said, "This is authentic according to the criteria of Muslim, and they did not record it." These and similar sayings testify that Allah, the Exalted and Most Honored, brought forth Adam's offspring from his loins and separated between the inhabitants of Paradise and those of the Fire. Extract from *Tafsir ibn Kathir*, in explanation of Qur'an 7:172.

[35] Ibn Kathir, *Tafsir ibn Kathir*, in explanation of Qur'an 3:82.

[36] Ibn Jawzi, *al-Wafa bi Ahwal ul-Mustafa*. This hadith is related on the authority of Maysara. [The original source is Imam ibn Abi Dunya in his *Manazil al-Ashraf*.]

[37] Ibn Kathir, *Tafsir ibn Kathir*, in explanation of Qur'an 3:82. He states it is also related by Tawus and Qatada.

[38] *Tafsir ibn Kathir*, in explanation of Qur'an 17:79.

[39] Amina, daughter of Wahb and mother of the Messenger of God, used to say that when she became pregnant with the Messenger of God, a voice told her: "You are pregnant with the lord of this nation; when he drops to the ground (in birth) say the words, 'I invoke for him the protection of the One God, from the evil of all who envy, from everyone committed to his oath and every prowling slave; may a champion protect me, for he is with the All-praised and All-glorious One, until I see him come into view.' And the proof of that is a light accompanying him that will fill the castles of Busra in Syria. And at his birth, then call him Muhammad, for in the Torah his name is "Ahmad" and the hosts of earth and heaven give him hamd, praise. In the Gospels his name is "Ahmad", the hosts of heaven and earth giving him hamd, praise. And his name in the Qur'an is "Muhammad", 'The praised one.' " Ibn Kathir, *The Life of the Prophet Muhammed* [*al-Sira al-Nabawiyya*], trans. Trevor Le Gassick (United Kingdom: Garnet Publishing, 1998), vol.1, p.147.

[40] This is related by Imam al-Hakim and Imam Ahmad ibn Hanbal. Ibn Rajab said, "The light that the mother of the Prophet saw emanating from her refers to the light that the Prophet brought in order to guide mankind and eradicate the darkness of shirk [polytheism]. Allah the Almighty says, ***'O People of the Scripture, there has come to you Our Messenger making clear to you much of what you used to conceal of the Scripture and overlooking much. There has come to you from Allah a light and a clear Book. By which Allah guides those who pursue His pleasure to the ways of peace and brings them out from darkness into the light, by His permission, and guides them to a straight path.'*** " (Q.5:15-16) Hafidh ibn Kathir said specifying al-Sham was an indication that the religion will be established there and this is why al-Sham will be, at the end of time, a fortress for Islam and the Muslims. Al-Sham will be the place where Isa, may Allah exalt his mention, will descend, in the white eastern lighthouse of Damascus. The Prophet said, *"A group of my ummah will remain victorious with the truth and not be harmed by anyone who forsakes them or anyone who disagrees with them, until the decree of Allah comes while they are as such."* (al-Bukhari and Muslim) The narration related by Imam al-Bukhari includes *"...And they will be in al-Sham."*

[41] The Bible – Deuteronomy (18:18).

[42] The Bible – Isaiah (29:12).

[43] Imam al-Bukhari, *Sahih*.

[44] Imam Sulami, *The Sufi book of Chivalry* [*Kitab al-Futuwwah*], trans. Shaykh Tosun Bayrak al-Jerrahi (New York: Inner Traditions International, 1983), p.34.

[45] Imam al-Bukhari, *Sahih*.

[46] Quote adapted from: ibn Kathir, *Bidayah wa al-Nihayah*, vol.2, p.470.

[47] Imam Ahmad ibn Hanbal, *Musnad*.

[48] Umm Salamah narrates, Sayyiduna Ali ibn Abi Talib, Allah ennoble his countenance, arrived in the company of the Prophet and the Prophet had already laid out a cloak. The Prophet, Ali, Fatimah, al-Hasan and al-Husayn sat on it. Then the Prophet got hold of the corners of the cloak, placed the corners over them and tied a knot. Then he said, *"O Allah! Be satisfied with them in the same manner as I am pleased with them."* This is narrated by Imam al-Tabarani.

[49]
Mary is hallowed in one line alone,
That she bore Jesus; Fatima in three.
For that she was the sweet delight of him
Who came a mercy to all living things,
Leader of former as of latter saints,
Who breathed new spirit into this dead world
And brought to birth the age of a New Law.

His lady she, who regal diadem
God's words adorn *Hath there come any time,*
The chosen one, resolver of knots
And hard perplexities, the Lion of God,
An emperor whose palace was a hut,
Accoutred with one sword, one coat of mail.
And she his mother, upon whom revolves
Love's compasses, the leader of Love's train,
That single candle in the corridor
Of sanctity resplendent, guardian
Of the integrity of that best race
Of all God's peoples; who, that the fierce flame
Of war and hatred might extinguished be,
Trod underfoot the crown and royal ring.
His mother too, the lord of all earth's saints
And strong right arm of every freeborn man,
Husain, the passion in the song of life,
Teacher of freedom to God's chosen few.
The character, the essential purity
Of holy children from their mothers come.

Muhammad Iqbal, *The Mystries of Selflessness* [*Rumuz-I Bekhudi*], trans. A.J. Arberry (Great Britain: John Murray (Publishers) Ltd, 1953), pp.65-66. Extract from the poem *That the Lady Fatima is the Perfect Pattern of Muslim Womanhood.*

[50] Shaykh al-Mutaqqi al-Hindi, *Kanz al-Umal*. It is also said that Sayyidah Fatimah was also named after Sayyidah Khadijah's mother Fatimah.

[51] The historian ibn Athir said, "Sayyiduna Ali ibn Abi Talib, was the first caliph both of whose parents were pure Hashimites. He was so judicial minded that he could not put up with the dishonesty of his relations or friends, and was so much engrossed in piety that at the time of his marriage with Sayyidah Fatimah he did not possess anything except a camel skin on which he fed his camels in the day, and which he converted into a bed sheet at night. The Prophet in his table talk has not extolled any one of his companions as much as he has Ali and one must know that Sayyiduna Ali never spoke a lie during his lifetime."

[52] Sayyidah Khadijah is the daughter of Khuwaylid of the Abd al-Uzza clan of the tribe of Quraysh and her mother, Fatimah al-Za'idah, from the tribe of Amir ibn Lu'ayy clan, also of the Quraysh.

[53] Ahmad ibn Zayni Dahlan al-Shafi al-Makki, *Seerah al-Nabawiyyah*, p.176.

[54] A huge fight erupted between the tribes as to who would have the honor to re-build it. They all decided the best way to avoid bloodshed was for all of the tribes to build it together. It was at this same time, around 605 C.E, that a leader from the Quraysh by the name of Walid ibn al-Mughirah heard news of a ship from the Byzantine Empire that had high grade construction materials being imported from Egypt to be sent to al-Habasha to restore one of their Grand Churches. He, being one of the richest men of the area, made the journey to the port of Shuayba, near modern day Jeddah, where the ship was docked. He knew this was his best chance to obtain these materials that may never be so easily available again. He not only purchased the materials, but he also hired one of the lead carpenters to travel to Makkah to be the head of construction for the Ka'bah. As the Ka'bah was being repaired, all of the tribes worked hard and helped in any way they could. The Prophet Muhammad himself worked alongside his uncle Abbas. One day, while rebuilding, more fights started among the various tribes as the time had now come to place the blessed black stone (*Hajar al-Aswad*) in its place. It had become so intense that the tribes were getting ready to duel with each other for the

honor. Imam ibn Hisham tells us that, "In order to ease tensions, Abu Umayyah ibn al-Mughirah, another leader among the Quraysh, suggested that the decision of the first person who enters from the Banu Shayba gate of the Ka'bah should be binding". The Quraysh agreed to this proposal and then they all waited with anxious excitement for the person who would enter the gate. All praise is due to Allah, the first person to enter the gate was none other than the Prophet Muhammad ibn Abdullah. They all shouted out in joy. "Yes, there he is, truly he is al-Amin, the trustworthy one. Muhammad, Muhammad, the trustworthy one." The Prophet then proposed that the black stone be put on a cloth with each tribal leader taking hold of the cloth, then when it was time to place the stone in, he himself would do it. When the time came, he placed the stone in its place and all were happy. The Prophet therefore prevented bloodshed. Allah says, ***"whoever saves the life of a person is as if he has saved the the whole of humankind."*** (Q.5:32)

[55] The saying in the quotation is from *al-Majmu*. Imam Malik narrated in the *Muwatta*, from more than one of those whom he trusted that Sa'd ibn Abi Waqqas and Sa'id ibn Zayd ibn Amr ibn Nufayl died in al-Aqeeq and were carried to Madinah and buried there. Yusuf ibn Abd al-Barr said in his *al-Istidhkar*, "The report to that effect from Sa'd and Sa'd, as was narrated by Imam Malik ibn Anas, and it is authentic [*sahih*]." In *Fath al-Bari* Hafidh ibn Hajar said, "There was a difference of opinion as to whether it is permissible to transport the deceased from one land to another. It was said that it is disliked, because it involves delaying the burial and exposing him to transgression of his sanctity. And it was said that it is recommended. Rather, it depends: It is not allowed if there is no clear purpose, such as burying him in good places. The ruling on it being disliked varies, and it may reach the level of being prohibited. It is recommended if one is close to a virtuous place, as Imam Abu Idris al-Shafi stated that it is recommended to transport the deceased to a virtuous place, such as Makkah and elsewhere."

[56] Imam Muslim, *Sahih*. Narrated on the authority of Bara ibn Azib.

[57] Imam al-Bayhaqi, *Sunan al-Kubra*. Narrated on the authority of Jabir ibn Abdullah.

[58] Imam al-Bukhari, *Sahih*.

[59] Imam al-Tirmidhi, *Shamail Muhammadiyyah*.

[60] Imam Ahmad ibn Hanbal, *Musnad*. Narrated on the authority of Anas ibn Malik.

[61] Imam al-Hakim, *Mustadrak*. Narrated on the authority of Anas ibn Malik's mother. In regard to the features of Sayyiduna Ali ibn Abi Talib, it is related that Sayyiduna Ali had a splendid face, as if it was the full moon, his neck appeared like a silver jug and whenever he smiled, his teeth appeared to be organized pearls. Among the virtues of Sayyidah Fatimah al-Zahrah is that her husband was hand picked by Allah and his Messenger.

[62] ***"And his wives are their mothers."*** (Q.33:6) Imam al-Samarqand says in his *Tafsir al-Qur'an*, " ***'His wives are their mothers'***, meaning the prohibition like that of their mothers." Imam Jalal al-Din al-Suyuti in his *Tafsir al-Jalalayn*, explaining the verse, says, "This is forbidding any marriage with them." In *Tafsir al-Qurtubi*, it states that Qatada said, "a man (Talha ibn Ubaydullah) said, 'If the Messenger of Allah passes away, I would marry Aisha.' Hence Allah revealed, ***'Nor is it right for you that you should annoy the Messenger of Allah,'*** then revealed, ***'and his wives are their mothers.'*** " In *Tafsir ibn Kathir* it states, "It was reported from Imam Zayn al-Abidin the son of Imam al-Husayn, who narrated from Muhammad son of Abi Hamad, from Mahran, from Sufyan, from Dawud son of Abi Hind, from Ikrimah, from ibn Abbas, that the saying, ***'And it is not lawful for you to bother the Messenger of Allah.'*** He said, 'It was speaking to a man that desired to marry some of the women of the Prophet.' A man said to Sufyan, 'Is it Aisha?' He replied 'They mentioned that.' "

[63] The entire hadith is related by Imam Abu Dawud, *Sunan Abu Dawud*; Imam al-

Tirmidhi, *Sunan.*

[64] Imam ibn Abi Shaybah, *al-Musannaf.* Many other Imams related different versions of this hadith, among them are Imam al-Bukhari, Muslim, al-Bayhaqi, al-Hakim, al-Tabarani, al-Daylami and others.

[65] This is related by Imam Ahmad ibn Hanbal, Imam al-Tabarani, Nur al-Din al-Haythami al-Shafi, Imam Abu Nuaym. Shamsuddin al-Dhahabi, ibn Hajar al-Asqalani and ibn Kathir also relate this narration.

[66] This is related by Imam al-Hakim, Imam ibn Hibban, Imam ibn Asakir in his *al-Tarikh,* and others who say it is on the authority of Caliph Umar ibn al-Khattab.

[67] Imam ibn Hibban, *Sahih ibn Hibban;* Imam al-Hakim, *Mustadrak;* Imam al-Bukhari, *al-Adab al-Mufrad.* This hadith is authentic on the authority of Aisha al-Siddiqah. Hafidh ibn Hajar al-Asqalani proved this was related by Imams Abu Dawud and al-Tirmidhi and they deemed it as good [*hasan*], while Imam ibn Hibban and al-Hakim declared the hadith to be authentic [*sahih*].

[68] Imam al-Hakim, *Mustadrak;* Imam al-Muhibb al-Tabari, *Dhakhair al-Uqba fi Manaqib Dhaw al-Qurba;* Qadi al-Shawkani, *Durr al-Sahabah Fi Manaqib al-Qarabah wal-Sahabah.*

[69] Imam al-Tirmidhi, *Sunan,* and it is an authentic hadith narrated on the authority of Abu Hurayrah.

[70] Imam ibn Hibban, *Sahih ibn Hibban,* and is on the authority of Sayyidah Aisha al-Siddiqah.

[71] Imam Abu Nu'aym, *Hilyat al-Awliyah;* Imam Jalal al-Din al-Suyuti in *Tafsir al-Durr al-Manthur.*

[72] Imam al-Hakim, *Mustadrak.*

[73] Abu Hamid al-Ghazali, *The Alchemy of Happiness* (USA: Great Books of the Islamic World, Inc., distributed by KAZI Publications, second ed. 2008), vol.1, p.261.

[74] Imam al-Hakim, *Mustadrak.*

[75] Imam Abu Nu'aym, *Hilyat al-Awliyah;* Imam Jalal al-Din al-Suyuti, *Tafsir al-Durr al-Manthur.*

[76] This is the revelation of the first Surah, al-Alaq.

[77] The dowry of the Prophet's wives was five-hundred *dirhams* each, which is equivalent to one-hundred and thirty riyaals today. And his daughters were married for the mahr of four-hundred dinaars, which is equivalent to one-hundred riyaals today. Allah, the Most High, said, ***"Indeed in the Messenger of Allah you have a most beautiful example to follow."*** (Q.33:21)

[78] "The Prophet was then twenty-five years of age when he married Sayyidah Khadijah. She is said to have been 40 years of age with some disagreement among the scholars. Allah Knows best. In regard to the blessed marriage; the two uncles of the Prophet, Hamzah and Abu Talib, approached her uncle, Umar ibn Asad, with the formal proposal. It was accepted and the two families began preparing for the wedding. Halimah al-Sa'diyyah, who nursed the Prophet in his infancy, was specially invited for the wedding and travelled to Makkah from her village. When she left after the festivities, Sayyidah Khadijah presented her with household goods, a camel and forty goats as an expression of gratitude to the lady who had taken such good care of (Sayyiduna) Muhammad in his infancy." Extract from: Mahmood Ahmad Ghadanfar, *The Great Women of Islam,* trans. Jamila Muhammad Qawi (Riyadh, Saudi Arabia: Darussalam, 2003), p.25.

[79] She had already learned about the teachings of Ibrahim, Musa and Isa from her cousin Waraqah ibn Nawfal.

[80] Ibn Kathir, *The Life of the Prophet Muhammed,* trans. Le Gassick, vol.1, p.279.

[81] Imam Ahmad ibn Hanbal, *Musnad*.

[82] It is related by Imam al-Bukhari in his *Sahih*, on the authority of Abu Hurayrah, "Jibreel came to the Prophet and said, 'O! Messenger of Allah! This is Khadijah, coming to you with a dish having meat soup (or some food or drink). When she reaches you, greet her on behalf of her Lord (Allah) and on my behalf, and give her the glad tidings of having a palace made of Qasab in Paradise, wherein there will be neither any noise nor any toil.' "

[83] Sir John Glubb, *The Life and Times of Mohammed* (New York: Stein and Day, 1970).

[84] This is related by Imam Ahmad ibn Hanbal, Imam Abu Hatim, Imam al-Tabari and many others.

[85] Ibn Kathir, *The Life of the Prophet Muhammed*, trans. Le Gassick, vol.2, pp.33-34; *Tafsir al-Kashaf*; Imam Jalal al-Din al-Suyuti, *Tafsir Durr al-Manthur; Tafsir Ruh al-Ma'ani; Tafsir Jalalayn.*

[86] Ibn Ishaq, *The Life of Muhammad: A Translation of ibn Ishaq's Sirat Rasul Allah*, trans. Alfred Guillaume (Karachi: Oxford University Press, 1967; repr. 2013), p.164.

[87] Ibn Kathir, *The Life of the Prophet Muhammed*, trans. Le Gassick, vol.2, pp.35-36.

[88] Imam Ahmad related that Abdullah ibn Umar said, "I watched the Prophet for a month and he would recite in the two cycles before the morning prayer. ***'Say: O you who disbelieve!'*** and, ***'Say: He is Allah, One.'*** " (Q.112:1) This was also recorded by Imam al-Tirmidhi, Imam ibn Majah and Imam al-Nasa'i. Imam al-Tirmidhi said, "This is a good hadith."

[89] They not only mocked the Prophet but also physically attacked the Prophet and the Muslims. In the early days of Islam, there came a point when Sayyiduna Abu Bakr al-Siddique, Allah be pleased with him, could not find it in himself to keep the beauty of Islam a secret anymore. He would recite the Qur'an loudly in his yard and would at times give public declarations of his love of Islam. One day, Abu Bakr went to the Ka'bah, alongside the Prophet and other believers and made one of the first public declarations of Islam. He pleaded with the people of Makkah to believe in one God and to accept Muhammad as the Messenger of Allah. In the middle of his speech, Utbah ibn Rabiah and others jumped on Abu Bakr and started to beat him half to death. In fact, everyone around the Ka'bah thought Abu Bakr was dead due to both of his eyes being swollen and shut. This made his tribe, the Banu Tamim, infuriated and they vowed that if Abu Bakr died they were going to go to Utbah's house to kill him and everyone who tried to stop them. When Sayyiduna Abu Bakr did finally wake up, to the surprise of everyone, all he kept saying was, "How is the Prophet?" He immediately refused any personal help and went straight to the Prophet's house to see if he was well. The Prophet, who had been attacked as well, was rescued in the process by his own tribe, Banu Hashim, who would continuously protect and secure his personal safety during the first years of the mission. The events can be found related in ibn Kathir's *The Life of the Prophet Muhammed*, trans. Le Gassick, vol.1, pp.319-320.

[90] Imam al-Bukhari, *Sahih*.

[91] This is related by ibn Kathir in his *Tafsir* in explanation of Qur'an, Surah 111.

[92] Imam al-Tabari, *Tarikh al-Rusul wa'l-Muluk*, vol.39, p.163.

[93] Imam ibn Sa'd, *The Women of Madina*, trans. Aisha Bewley (London: Ta-Ha Publishers, 1995), p.26. [This is a partial translation of *Tabaqat ibn Sa'd*.]

[94] Hind ibn Abi Hala was Sayyidah Khadija's son from a previous marriage. Watt, W. Montgomery, *Khadidja* (Encyclopaedia of Islam, Second Edition), Edited by: P. Bearman, Th. Bianquis, C.E. Bosworth, E. van Donzel, W.P. Heinrichs. http://dx.doi.org/10.1163/1573-3912_islam_SIM_4116. Accessed 10 August 2016. First published online: 2012. First print edition: ISBN: 9789004161214, 1960-2007.

[95] Imam ibn Hajar al-Asqalani, *al-Isabah.*

[96] The Messenger of Allah ﷺ is known to have said, *"If I had ten daughters I would marry them all to Uthman."* Imam al-Tabari, *al-Mu'jam al-Kabir*. The Prophet said this out of love and because of Uthman's kindness, modesty and general good conduct.

[97] Ibn Kathir, *The Life of the Prophet Muhammed*, trans. Le Gassick, vol.2, p.325.

[98] Ibn Kathir, *The Life of the Prophet Muhammed*, trans. Le Gassick, vol.2, pp.347-348. Shortly before the conquest of Makkah, Abu al-Aas was captured by the Muslims while he was returning from Syria trading goods belonging to various Qurayshi businessmen. Sayyidah Zaynab offered him security, as a result of which he was released by the Muslims. Abu al-Aas took all the trading goods to Makkah and handed them over to the owners. Once he had discharged his duty, he declared his Islam to the people of Makkah and made his way to Madinah, where he was reunited with his beloved wife, Sayyidah Zaynab.

[99] Ibn Ishaq, *The Life of Muhammad*, trans. Guillaume, p.146.

[100] Ibn Ishaq, *The Life of Muhammad*, trans. Guillaume, p.152. Ibn Kathir narrates: "When Abu Talib saw Quraysh engaged in this he wrote to the Negus some verses urging him to act with justice and kindness towards those of his people who were living with him:

> *'would that I knew how it is so far off for Jafar and Amr, and it is relatives who can be the most bitter enemies.*
>
> *And whether the actions of the Negus towards Jafar and his companions are still kind, or whether some mischief-maker has hindered that.*
>
> *You should know, may you avoid disaster, that you are noble, and that no alien would have complaint to you.*
>
> *We know that God has given you much abundance, and that the means of all goodness is attached to you.'* "

Quote from: Ibn Kathir, *The Life of the Prophet Muhammed*, trans. Le Gassick, vol.2, pp.16-17.

[101] Ibn Ishaq, *The Life of Muhammad*, trans. Guillaume, p.144.

[102] Imam al-Tabari, *Tarikh al-Tabari.*

[103] The events can be found narrated in: Ibn Ishaq, *The Life of Muhammad*, trans. Guillaume, pp.119-120; Ibn Kathir, *The Life of the Prophet Muhammed*, trans. Le Gassick, vol.1, p.345.

[104] Imam ibn Hisham, *Seerah ibn Hisham.*

[105] The events can be found narrated in: Ibn Ishaq, *The Life of Muhammad*, trans. Guillaume, p.119; Ibn Kathir, *The Life of the Prophet Muhammed*, trans. Le Gassick, vol.1, p.344.

[106] Imam al-Tabari, *Tarikh al-Tabari.*

[107] A full account can be found in: Ibn Ishaq, *The Life of Muhammad*, trans. Guillaume, p.117-118; Imam al-Tabari, *Tarikh al-Tabari*; Imam al-Bayhaqi, *Dala'il an-Nubuwwah*; Imam Jalal al-Din al-Suyuti, *al-Durr al-Manthur.*

[108] Ibn Ishaq, *The Life of Muhammad*, trans. Guillaume, p.145; Ibn Kathir, *The Life of the Prophet Muhammed*, trans. Le Gassick, vol.1, p.358.

[109] Imam al-Bukhari, *Sahih*; Imam Muslim, *Sahih*. They both relate this story and mention the supplication of the Prophet for Allah's blessing.

[110] Imam al-Bukhari, *Sahih*; Imam Muslim, *Sahih.*

[111] Dr. Muhammad Tahir ul-Qadri, *Fatimah, the Great Daughter of Prophet Muhammad*

(London: Minhaj-ul-Qur'an Publications, 2014), p.60. This is related by Imam al-Hakim, Imam Abu Ya'la, Imam al-Tabarani and others.

[112] This is related by Imam al-Tabarani; also recorded by Imam al-Bukhari, Imam al-Tirmidhi and Imam al-Nasa'i in their chapters on the explanation of the Qur'an – on the authority of Abdullah ibn Abbas.

[113] This is related by Imam al-Tirmidhi on the authority of Abdullah ibn Abbas and is a sound narration.

[114] The verse in question: "***He indeed led me astray from the Reminder (this Qur'an) after it had come to me. And Shaitan (Satan) is ever a deserter to man in the hour of need.***" (Q.25:20)

[115] Imam Abu Dawud records in his *Sunan* that both Uqbah and al-Nadir ibn al-Harith were defeated by Sayyiduna Ali in battle at Badr, and Allah knows best.

[116] Imam Muslim, *Sahih.*

[117] Imam Ahmad ibn Hanbal, *Musnad.*

[118] This is related by Imam ibn Hisham, Imam ibn Ishaq, Imam ibn Kathir, Imam Jalal al-Din al-Suyuti and others.

[119] Imam ibn Hisham, *Seerah ibn Hisham.*

[120] Ibn Ishaq, *The Life of Muhammad,* trans. Guillaume, p.172.

[121] Ibn Kathir, *The Life of the Prophet Muhammed,* trans. Le Gassick, vol.2, p.32.

[122] Ibn Kathir, *The Life of the Prophet Muhammed,* trans. Le Gassick, vol.2, p.172.

[123] Mahmood Ahmad Ghadanfar, *The Great Women of Islam,* trans. Qawi, pp.152-153.

[124] Sayyidi Ahmad ibn Ajiba states, "... certainly after the harshness and rough treatment you experienced from the idolaters there shall come ease, for Allah shall make you triumphant over them and you shall overcome them." He also explains the reason Allah mentions the word ease twice in relation to the same incident is because with every hardship (singular) "there comes two eases." Ahmad ibn Ajiba, *Prophetic Grace: The Qur'anic Merits of the Prophet Muhammad,* trans. Abdul Aziz Suraqah (USA: al-Madina Institute, 2012), pp.102-103. [This translation being excerpts from *al-Bahr al-Madid* by ibn Ajiba.]

[125] Muhammad Husayn Haykal, *The Life of the Prophet Muhammad,* trans. Ismail Raji al Faruqi (Malaysia: Islamic Book Trust, rev. edn. 2008), pp.128-129.

[126] Haykal, *The Life of the Prophet Muhammad,* trans. Faruqi, p.150.

[127] This is related by Imam Ahmad ibn Hanbal, Imam al-Tabarani, Nur al-Din al-Haythami al-Shafi, Imam Abu Nuaym. Shamsuddin al-Dhahabi, ibn Hajar al-Asqalani and ibn Kathir also relate this narration.

[128] In *Aqeedah Tahawiyyah* Imam al-Tahawi says, "The Pool [*al-Hawd*] that God honoured him with as solace for his community is real." In *Kitab Usul al-Deen* of the Shehu Uthman ibn Fodio, the same is said. In fact, any proper Aqeedah book from the Ahlus Sunnah will show that the Pond of Kawthar is true. The exact story is that the leaders of the Quraysh – al-As ibn Wa'il, Abu Jahl, Uqbah ibn Abi Mu'ayt and Ka'b ibn al-Ashraf – were laughing at the Prophet after the death of his three sons and especially Sayyiduna al-Qasim, the Peace of Allah be upon them. They would chase after the Prophet and call him abtar (the one who is cut off) and thus Allah revealed that those among Quraysh who were against the Prophet were the ones who were cut off. The truth of this is most of them passed away during the first few battles of Islam.

[129] Imam Ahmad ibn Hajar al-Haytami, *al-Sawaiq al-Muhariqah*; also related with similar wording by Imam al-Hakim, *Mustadrak*; Shaykh Muttaqqi al-Hindi, *Kanz al-Umal,* and by others.

[130] Imam al-Tabari, *Tafsir Rul al-Ma'ani.*

[131] Imam al-Tabarani, *al-Mujam al-Kabir;* Imam al-Hakim, *Mustadrak;* Imam Abu Nu'aym, *Hilyat al-Awliyah* and Imam al-Bazzar, *al-Musnad.*

[132] Recorded by Imam al-Tabarani, Abu Ya'la, Imam al-Daylami, Khatib al-Baghdadi, Nur al-Din al-Haythami al-Shafi, al-Mizzi and al-Sahhawi. Also related by Imam al-Hakim in his *Mustadrak,* on the authority of Jabir ibn Abdullah.

[133] Quba is where the Messenger of Allah built the first Masjid of Islam.

[134] Imam al-Bukhari, *Sahih.*

[135] Imam al-Tirmidhi, *Shamail Muhammadiyyah.*

[136] Imam al-Bukhari, *Sahih;* Imam Muslim, *Sahih.*

[137] Abu Ayyub al-Ansari is from the Banu an-Najjar. His full name is Khalid ibn Zayd ibn Kulayb.

[138] Imam al-Bukhari, *Sahih.*

[139] Sayyid Muhammad ibn Alawi al-Maliki, *Muhammad the Perfect Man,* trans. by Khalid Williams (Visions of Reality, 2013), p.157.

[140] Imam al-Tirmidhi, *Sunan;* Imam al-Hakim, *Mustadrak.* Imam al-Hakim and Imam al-Dhahabi have graded this hadith as authentic.

[141] Imam al-Tabarani, *al-Mujam al-Kabir* and *al-Awsat.* Also related by Imam Ahmad ibn Hanbal. Narrated on the authority of Abdullah ibn Abbas.

[142] Imam ibn Hibban, *Sahih ibn Hibban.* Narrated on the authority of Sayyidah Aisha al-Siddiqah.

[143] Imam ibn Asakir, *Tarikh ibn Asakir.*

[144] Imam ibn Majah, *Sunan.* Narrated on the authority of Sayyidah Aisha al-Siddiqah.

[145] Imam al-Bukhari, *Sahih.*

[146] In *al-Fusus al-Hikam* of ibn Arabi, he relates that the Prophet, "began by mentioning women and ended with the prayer. That is because woman is part of man in the root of the manifestation of her source, and man's recognition of himself preceded his recognition of his Lord. His recognition of his Lord is a result of his recognition of himself. For that reason, he said, peace be upon him: *'Whoever recognises himself, recognises his Lord.'* " Shaykh ibn Arabi, *The Seals of Wisdom* [*Fusus al-Hikam*], trans. Aisha Abd al-Rahman at-Tarjumana (Cape Town: Madinah Press, 2005), p.193.

[147] Imam al-Nasa'i, *Sunan al-Nasa'i;* Imam Ahmad ibn Hanbal, *Musnad.* It has been authenticated by Imam al-Hakim in his *Mustadrak* and by Imam ibn Hajar al-Asqalani in his *Fath al-Bari.*

[148] Hafidh ibn Hajar al-Asqalani explains, "The 'sweetness of one's eyes' is the beloved that one hopes never to depart from, the bliss that this beloved brings and the happiness that it enriches one's life with. This is experienced with prayer only by those who are reverently patient."

[149] Imam Muslim, *Sahih.* Related on the authority of Abu Hurayrah.

[150] Imam al-Tirmidhi, *Sunan.*

[151] Imam al-Tirmidhi, *Sunan;* also recorded by Imam al-Tabarani and Imam al-Bayhaqi.

[152] Imam al-Bukhari, *Sahih;* Imam Muslim, *Sahih.*

[153] Imam al-Tabari, *Tafsir al-Tabari.*

[154] Imam Muslim, *Sahih.*

[155] This is the opinion of ibn Abbas as related by ibn Kathir in his *Tafsir.*

[156] This statement of ibn Abbas is related by Imam al-Qurtubi in *Tafsir al-Qurtubi*.

[157] This was the view of Imam al-Tabari ibn Jarir, found in his *Tafsir*.

[158] This is also related by ibn Hajar al-Asqalani and Imam Munawi.

[159] This is a statement of Shaykh Dr. Muhammad Tahir al-Qadiri in his introduction to The Virtues of Sayyidah Fatimah.

[160] Imam al-Tabari, *Riyad al-Nadirah*, vol.3, p.109.

[161] Al-Qadi al-Qudai, *A Treasury of Virtues*, trans. Tahera Qutbuddin (New York: New York University Press, 2013), p.217.

[162] This is related in the *Ghurar al-Hikam*, p.82.

[163] Imam al-Hakim, *Mustadrak*; Imam al-Tabarani, *Mujam al-Kabir*; Imam Abu Nu'aym, *Hilyat al-Awliyah*, and others.

[164] Imam al-Tirmidhi, *Sunan*.

[165] Imam al-Hakim, *Mustadrak*.

[166] Imam al-Hakim, *Mustadrak*; Imam al-Tabarani, *Mujam al-Awsat*, narrated on the authority of Abdullah ibn Umar.

[167] Imam al-Tirmidhi, *Sunan*.

[168] Imam al-Bukhari, *Sahih*.

[169] Imam al-Bukhari, *Sahih*.

[170] Imam ibn Hajar al-Asqalani, *Fath al-Bari*.

[171] Khatib al-Baghdadi, *Tarikh al-Baghdad*; also related by Imam Jalal al-Din al-Suyuti. Wahhab al-Sharani relates something similar in his Yawaqit wal-Jawahir.

[172] Imam al-Bayhaqi, *Sunan al-Kubra*.

[173] This is related by Muhyidin ibn Arabi in his *Futuhat al-Makkiyyah*, Imam Abdul Wahhab al-Sharani relates something similar in his *Yawaqit wal-Jawahir*.

[174] Imam Muslim, *Sahih*.

[175] This comparison to Isa is very important, because it is as if the Messenger of Allah was telling him something. Meaning to live the example of the life of Isa, which if you look at it, he did. So much so, that even some around him looked at him as a god, while others spoke of their displeasure that the revelation did not come down to Ali. It was a very trying time for Sayyiduna Ali.

[176] Imam Ahmad ibn Hanbal, *Musnad*.

[177] Imam al-Tirmidhi, *Sunan*; Imam Ahmad ibn Hanbal, *Musnad*.

[178] Imam al-Bukhari, *Sahih*.

[179] Qadi Iyad, *Muhammad Messenger of Allah, Ash-Shifa of Qadi Iyad*, trans. Aisha Bewley (Norwich: Diwan Press, rev. edn. 2011), p.225.

[180] Qadi Iyad, *Muhammad Messenger of Allah, Ash-Shifa of Qadi Iyad*, trans. Aisha Bewley, pp.223-224.

[181] Imam Abu Nu'aym, *Hilyat al-Awliyah*; Imam Jalal al-Din al-Suyuti, *Tafsir al-Durr al-Manthur*.

[182] Imam al-Tabarani, *Mujam al-Kabir*; Imam al-Hakim, *Mustadrak*; Imam Abu Nu'aym, *Hilyat al-Awliyah*; Imam ibn Asakir, *Tarikh ibn Asakir*.

[183] Imam Ahmad ibn Hanbal, *Musnad*.

[184] Al-Waqidi, *Kitab al-Maghazi*.

[185] Imam ibn Sa'd, *al-Tabaqat ibn Sa'd*.

[186] Imam Abu Dawud, *Sunan.*

[187] Haykal, *The Life of the Prophet Muhammad,* trans. Faruqi, p.283.

[188] Imam al-Hakim, *Mustadrak.*

[189] Imam al-Hakim, *Mustadrak;* Imam al-Bayhaqi, *Sunan al-Bayhaqi;* and Imam al-Tabari.

[190] Imam al-Bukhari, *Sahih.*

[191] Imam al-Bukhari, *Sahih.*

[192] Imam Jalal al-Din al-Suyuti, *Tarikh al-Khulafa.*

[193] Imam ibn Hajar al-Haytami, *al-Sawaiq al-Muhariqah.*

[194] Jalal Uddin Rumi, *Mathnawi,* trans. R. A. Nicholson (Konya: Konya Metropolitan Municipality, 2011), vol.1, pp.289-290. Sayyiduna Ali's response is found on p.294.

[195] Ibn Rushd said, "Glancing at a woman prior to proposal was permitted by Malik up to the face and hands alone, while others permitted the whole body except the private parts. Some have prohibited this without qualification. Abu Hanifa permitted glancing at the feet along with the face and hands. The reason for their disagreement is that the command permits glancing at women in general terms and the proscription also prohibits it in general terms. It is also laid down in qualified terms, that is, glancing at the face and hands, which was the interpretation of most jurists of the words of the Exalted, ***"[Women] are not to display their adornment save that which is apparent"*** (Q.24:32), that they mean the face and the hands. Further, there is the analogy of the permissibility, according to the majority, of uncovering them during hajj. Those who forbade the use of this principle did so because of the absolute prohibition of looking at women." Muhammad ibn Ahmad ibn Rushd, *The Distinguished Jurist's Primer,* trans. Imran A. K. Nyazee (Reading: Garnet Publishing Ltd, 1996), vol.2, p.2. Imam al-Nawawi said, "When (a man) wants to marry (a woman), it is *mustahabb* (preferable) for him to look at her so that he will have no regrets. According to another view, it is not preferable but it is allowed. The first view is correct because of the ahadith, and it is permitted to look repeatedly, with or without her permission. If it is not easy to look at her, he may send a woman to check her out and describe her to him. A woman may also look at a man if she wants to marry him, for she will like in him what he likes in her. What is permissible for him to look at is the face and hands, front and back. He should not look at anything else." *Rawdat al-Talibin wa Umdatul-Mufteen.* "Imam Ahmad said: 'He is to look at her face and this is not to be done lustfully or out of pleasure. He has the right to look more than once and to observe her beauty because the goal cannot be achieved except through this.' Imam al-Shafi said: 'He is to look at her face and hands.' Then he mentioned the story of Umar ibn al-Khattab when he proposed to the daughter of Ali ibn Abi Talib (Umm Kulthum). Ali sent her to Umar for him to look at her and Umar was pleased with what he saw and as she was walking away Umar looked at her shin and she said to him: 'If it wasn't for the fact that you were the Leader of the Believers I would hit you in both of your eyes!' " *Al-Mughni.*

[196] Rumi, *Mathnawi,* trans. Nicholson, vol.1, p.294.

[197] Shaykh Abd al-Qadir al-Jilani, *Secret of Secrets,* trans. Shaykh Tosun Bayrak al-Jerrahi, p16.

[198] The version of events described has been adapted from many narrations including those found within the *Hilyat al-Awliyah; Siyar A'lam al-Nubala; Seerah ibn Hisham; Seerah ibn Ishaq; Tafsir ibn Kathir; Fath al-Bari; Sunan al-Kubra; Dala'il al-Bayhaqi.*

[199] Shaikh Abdal-Hakim Murad, *The Sunna as Primordiality,* http://masud.co.uk/ISLAM/ahm/sunnah.htm. Accessed on 03 November 2017.

[200] Imam al-Hakim, *Mustadrak;* Imam al-Nasa'i, *Khasais al-Nasa'i.*

[201] Imam ibn Majah, *Sunan.* This is related on the authority of Abdullah ibn Abbas, and

said it was good on the condition set by Imam Muslim, this is agreed upon by Imam al-Dhahabi and Imam al-Bayhaqi; Imam al-Tabarani and others say it is an authentic narration [*sahih*].

[202] Imam ibn Majah, *Sunan*.

[203] Imam al-Bukhari, *Sahih*.

[204] Imam al-Qurtubi, *Tafsir al-Qurtubi*.

[205] This was related by many scholars including ibn Hajar al-Asqalani in his *Lisan al-Mizan* and *Tahdhib al-Tahdhib*.

[206] Imam Abu Nu'aym, *Hilyat al-Awliyah*.

[207] Imam Ahmad ibn Hanbal, *Musnad*.

[208] Williams, *The Perfect Family – Virtues of the Ahl al-Bayt*, p.82. [Chapter: *The Virtues of Lady Fatimah* by ibn Shahin.]

[209] Imam Muslim, *Sahih*; Imam ibn Majah, *Sunan*.

[210] Imam ibn Hajar al-Haytami, *Sawaiq al-Muhariqah*.

[211] Dr. Muhammad Tahir ul-Qadri, *Fatimah, the Great Daughter of Prophet Muhammad*, p.82. This is related by Imam al-Tabari in his *Dhakhair al-Uqba fi Manaqib Dhaw al-Qurba*.

[212] Imam al-Hakim, *Mustadrak*; Imam Ahmad ibn Hanbal, *Musnad*.

[213] Shaykh Abu Bakr al-Haythami, *Majma al-Zawaid*.

[214] Imam Ahmad ibn Hanbal, *Musnad*.

[215] Imam Ibn Majah, *Sunan*.

[216] Imam al-Nasa'i, *Sunan al-Nasa'i*. Other narrations also mention: blankets, two millstones, and a waterskin with two jugs.

[217] This is related by Imam al-Hakim and Imam al-Bayhaqi.

[218] This is related by Imam ibn Hibban.

[219] Imam al-Bukhari, *Sahih*.

[220] Imam Malik, *Muwatta*.

[221] Imam al-Bukhari, *Sahih*.

[222] Imam al-Nasa'i, *Sunan al-Nasa'i*.

[223] "Ali sold the shield to Uthman for 400 *dirhams* and as he was hurrying back to the Prophet to hand over the sum as mahr, Uthman stopped him and said: 'I am returning your shield to you as a present from me on your marriage to Fatimah.' " Abdul Wahid Hamid, *Companions of the Prophet* (Muslim Education & Literary Services, rev. edn. 1995), p.22.

[224] Imam al-Bukhari, *Sahih*.

[225] Imam al-Bukhari, *Sahih*.

[226] Imam Malik, *Muwatta*.

[227] Imam Malik, *Muwatta*.

[228] Imam ibn Majah, *Sunan*.

[229] Imam ibn Majah, *Sunan*.

[230] Imam Abu Dawud, *Sunan*.

[231] Imam al-Hakim, *Mustadrak*; Imam al-Bayhaqi, *Sunan al-Kubra*, on the authority of Abdullah ibn Umar.

[232] Imam Abu Dawud, *Sunan*; Imam ibn Majah, *Sunan*; Imam al-Hakim, *Mustadrak* and Imam al-Bayhaqi.

[233] This hadith is related by many Imams with various wordings: Imam al-Bukhari, *Sahih*; Imam Muslim, *Sahih*; Imam Abu Dawud, *Sunan*; Imam al-Tirmidhi, *Sunan*.

[234] The Provider, "is the one who created the means of sustenance as well as those who are sustained, and who conveys the means to the creatures as well as creating for them the ways of enjoying them. Sustaining is of two kinds: outward, consisting of nourishment and food, which is for the sake of what is outward, namely the body. Inwardly, it consists in things known and things revealed, and that is directed to our hearts and inmost parts. This latter is the higher of the two modes of sustenance, for its fruit is eternal life; while the fruit of external sustenance is bodily strength for a short period of time. God – great and glorious – Himself attends to creating the two modes of sustenance and is graciously disposed to convey both kinds, but ***He extends sustenance to whomever He wills and decrees*** (Q.42:12)." Abu Hamid al-Ghazali, *The Ninety-Nine Beautiful Names of God*, trans. David B. Burrell and Nazih Daher (Cambridge: Islamic Text Society, 1992), p.78.

[235] The Merciful, "The Mercy of God – great and glorious – is both perfect and inclusive: perfect inasmuch as it wants to fulfil the needs of those in need and does meet them; and inclusive inasmuch as it as it embraces both deserving and undeserving, encompassing this world and the next, and includes bare necessities and needs, and special gifts over and above them. So He is utterly and truly merciful." Al-Ghazali, *The Ninety-Nine Beautiful Names of God*, trans. Burrell and Daher, p.53.

[236] Imam Sulami, *The Sufi book of Chivalry*, trans. Shaykh Tosun Bayrak al-Jerrahi, pp.49-50.

[237] Imam Sulami, *The Sufi book of Chivalry*, trans. Shaykh Tosun Bayrak al-Jerrahi, p.77.

[238] Imam Abu Dawud, *Sunan*; Imam al-Hakim, *Mustadrak*: authenticated by Imam al-Dhahabi. People used to bury their daughters out of fear of poverty and dishonor.

[239] According to Imams Abu Hanifah, Ahmad ibn Hanbal and Malik ibn Anas, marriage is recommended, however for certain individuals it becomes obligatory [*Wajib*]. Imam al-Shafi considers it to be recommended or preferable.

[240] Imam ibn Majah, *Sunan*.

[241] Imam al-Tirmidhi, *Sunan*.

[242] Imam al-Bukhari, *Sahih*.

[243] Imam Muslim, *Sahih*.

[244] Imam Muslim, *Sahih*.

[245] Imam al-Tirmidhi, *Sunan*.

[246] This is a hadith that has many variations, the most famous being related by Imam al-Tirmidhi, *Sunan* and Imam ibn Majah, *Sunan*.

[247] Imam al-Bukhari, *Sahih*.

[248] Imam al-Tirmidhi, *Sunan*; also related by Imam ibn Majah and Imam al-Nasa'i.

[249] Imam al-Tirmidhi, *Sunan*. This hadith is narrated on the authority of Abdullah ibn Abbas.

[250] Imam al-Bayhaqi, *Sahih al-Jami*; also related by Imam Ahmad ibn Hanbal, Imam al-Tirmidhi and Imam ibn Majah.

[251] Imam al-Bukhari, *Sahih*; Imam Muslim, *Sahih*.

[252] Imam Ahmad ibn Hanbal, *Musnad*; Imam Abu Dawud, *Sunan*; Imam ibn Majah, *Sunan*.

[253] Imam al-Tirmidhi, *Sunan*.

[254] Imam al-Bukhari, *Sahih*; Imam Muslim, *Sahih*.

[255] Imam al-Bazzar recounts that a man was circumambulating the Ka'bah carrying his mother. The Prophet asked him, *"Have you repaid her?"* The man said, "No, not even for one of her moans" (i.e. one of the moans of labour, delivery and so on).

[256] Imam al-Tirmidhi, *Sunan*.

[257] Imam al-Bukhari, *Sahih*.

[258] Imam al-Hakim, *Mustadrak*.

[259] Imam Abu Dawud, *Sunan*.

[260] For a fuller account of this event see *The Virtues of Lady Fatimah* by ibn Shahin in: Williams, *The Perfect Family – Virtues of the Ahl al-Bayt*, pp.80-81.

[261] Williams, *The Perfect Family – Virtues of the Ahl al-Bayt*, p.75.

[262] Imam ibn Sa'd, *The Women of Madina*, trans. Aisha Bewley, p.19.

[263] Shaykh Muhyidin ibn Arabi said, "Praise belongs to Allah the Great; His Majesty [*Jalal*] is part of the manifestation of His Beauty [*Jamal*]." Shaykh ibn Arabi, *'On Majesty and Beauty'* [*Kitab al-Jalal wa-l Jamal*], trans. Rabia Terri Harris, in the Journal of the Muhyiddin ibn 'Arabi Society, Volume VIII (Oxford: Beshara Press, 1989), pp.5-32. Imam al-Tabari explains the statement [*Tahmeed*] when he said, "Alhamdulillah is a praise that Allah praised Himself with, indicating to His servants that they too should praise Him, as if Allah had said, Say: 'All thanks and praise is due to Allah.' It is said that the statement entails praising Allah by mentioning His most beautiful names and most honorable attributes. When one proclaims, 'All thanks are due to Allah,' he will be thanking Him for His favors and bounties." *Tafsir al-Tabari*.

[264] Imam al-Tirmidhi, *Sunan*.

[265] Imam al-Tirmidhi, *Sunan*. This hadith is narrated on the authority of Abdullah ibn Abbas.

[266] Imam al-Hakim, *Mustadrak*.

[267] Imam al-Daylami, *Musnad al-Firdaws*.

[268] Imam Tabarani, *Mu'jam al-Awsat*.

[269] Imam al-Hakim, *Mustadrak*.

[270] Related by Imam Muslim, Imam al-Tirmidhi and Imam Nasa'i.

[271] Imam al-Hakim, *Mustadrak*.